# MIRACLES
## OF
## JOHN PAUL II

Paweł Zuchniewicz

# MIRACLES
## OF
## JOHN PAUL II

Catholic Youth Studio - KSM Inc.

Polish Title: Cuda Jana Pawła II

Translation:
Paul Bulas, Fr. Ted Nowak OMI, Margaret Olszewski

Cover design:
Iwona Miśkiewicz,
Elżbieta Michalczak (English Edition)

Cover photo:
Getty Images

Photos:
L'Osservatore Romano; AFP; Getty Images; NASA;
Canadian Press (Abaca Press/Laurent Zabulon; John Gabb;
Lionel Cironneau; Action Press; Massimo Sambucetti;
Chao Soi Cheong; Pier Paolo Cito); KSM Archives;
Grzegorz Gałązka; Anna Rogala; Ryszard Rzepecki; Bill Wittman,
Tadeusz Woliński.

Technical Editing:
Anna Rogala

Corrections:
Fr. Chris Pulchny OMI,
Tom Urbaniak, PhD

Design and Electronic Layout:
Elżbieta Michalczak

ISBN 0-9780979-0-4

Publisher:
Catholic Youth Studio–KSM Inc.
183 Roncesvalles Ave.
Toronto, Ontario M6R 2L5
Canada
Tel. 416-588-0555
Fax: 416-588-9995
www.catholicradio.ca

Printing:
Drukarnia Wydawnicza im. W. L. Anczyca
30-011 Kraków, ul. Wrocławska 53
Poland

# Contents

# *Foreword*

**14 December 2005, 00:10.** That was the date and time displayed in the e-mail message I received from Fr. Marian Gil OMI, director of Catholic Youth Studio in Toronto. A few weeks earlier I had asked him and many others across Poland and all over the world to forward to me any testimonies he may have about extraordinary occurrences attributed to the person of John Paul II. I concluded my search for material – indeed, writing the book itself – once Fr. Gil sent me an e-mail with "A miracle has happened!" in the subject line. The text was written by a young Polish man named Konrad, living in Canada, who recounted his great love for Paulina, a young Polish woman also living in Canada. The two met near the end of 1999. A year later, they found out that Paulina had lymphoma.

*"We were all in shock and had no clue what to do," wrote Konrad. "Eventually, Paulina began to cry from the pain. The disease was advancing and the last resort was chemotherapy. We spent time with her every day at the oncology department of the hospital; we prayed that Paulina would be cured. Paulina lost her strength and all her hair. Those were terrible times for all of us."*

Then came World Youth Day 2002 and the visit of Pope John Paul II to Toronto.

*"Our entire family attended this wonderful event together with Paulina and our friends,"* recalled Konrad. *"We waited for two days under a bare sky for John Paul II. The weather was odd – windy, with intermittent rain – but we managed to*

*keep our spirits up by singing and talking among ourselves. As the Pope arrived, the dark clouds seemed to part and the sun shone down. We felt at that moment as though something incredible was happening. Paulina always dreamt of meeting the Pope. She had already seen him in Italy, where he even patted her on the head and exchanged a few words with her – she was four years old at the time. When Paulina saw the Pope now after so many years, she began to cry uncontrollably. With deep faith she offered her life and herself completely to him. We knew that the Holy Father had come to us, to Paulina, to heal her. A few days later we went with Paulina for more tests. A miracle happened! The cancer had disappeared – not a trace of it was left. From that time on, Paulina has undergone many additional tests, all of which have turned up no trace of the illness. We are elated that we can count on starting the family we wanted and that everything has returned to normal.*

*I wanted to share this testimony to help others; to give hope to those who have all but lost hope. Sometimes it's hard to recall that terrible period in our lives but maybe it's necessary so that we can thank God."*

This story was the last one to reach me but is the first testimony to appear in this book bearing witness to the conviction that John Paul II is a saint.

This book could never have been written without the help of the many people who agreed to share their testimonies and experiences. I therefore take this opportunity to thank all of them: Kay Kelly and Anthony Keegan of Great Britain; Franciszek Szechyński, Fr. Janusz Błażejak OMI, Fr. Marian Gil OMI, Rev. Jacek Nowak Tchr., Michael Valpy, Bill Taylor and Fr. Tom Rosica CSB (all from Canada). I also thank Fr. Mirosław Drozdek SAC of Zakopane (Krzeptówka), Rev. Paweł Ross of Ukraine and Mrs. Feliksa (Warsaw), Aleksandra Ludwikowska, Danuta and Stanisław Rybicki (Cracow), Rev. Michel Remery of Holland and Dr. Mark Kośmicki. I thank Dr. Patrick Theillier, director of the Medical Office in Lourdes; Bishop Tadeusz Pieronek of Cracow and Archbishop Tadeusz Kondrusiewicz in Moscow, for the interviews that appear in this book.

The testimonies span many situations and come from diverse areas of the world. The common thread to all these testimonies is the conviction that John Paul II had an intimate relationship with the Divine Mystery – not only by virtue of his position in the Church, but as a human being. This became especially clear when his earthly journey reached its conclusion.

Paweł Zuchniewicz

# Chapter 1.

## SANTO SUBITO

*C*hrist neither shortened his days nor did He save him from years of suffering through illness – yet never, not even in his final moments, did I ever hear him reproach God.

*In sickness and suffering – in everything that caused him pain, even the assassination attempt - John Paul II always saw God's will and God's goodness; he was able to see the greater good that God was preparing for him. I remember when he had to step away from the window not being able to speak to the faithful gathered at St. Peter's Square … he said, "Maybe it would be better that I die if I cannot fulfill my mission." Immediately after saying this, however, he added: "May Your will be done. Totus Tuus."*

*I looked at his life and was with him right until he entered God's house, and I testify that it was always like this – right up to his last heartbeat …*

*During the funeral ceremony, the wind closed page by page the Book of the Gospels that was placed upon the papal coffin … but it didn't close the book that this loyal Witness of Divine Truth and Love wrote in people's hearts, through his very life.*

Excerpt from the homily of Archbishop Stanisław Dziwisz
delivered at the shrine in Łagiewniki, Poland
October 16, 2005

# FROM THE VERY BEGINNING, THE PONTIFICATE OF JOHN PAUL II WAS FULL OF SURPRISES

The first surprise was the news that someone from "a faraway land" had been chosen as Pope. Many other surprises would follow. On October 16, 2005, in an interview shown on Polish television 27 years to the day after that papal election, the successor of John Paul II summed up the effects of the cardinals' election of Karol Wojtyła to the Throne of St. Peter.

"Through his public appearances, his presence, his ability to convey things anew, the Holy Father inspired and challenged us to be more sensitive about moral values and the importance of religion in the world," recalled Benedict XVI. "This led to a new opening, a renewed interest in religion and an awareness of the necessity of the religious dimension of the human being – but most of all, to an increase in the authority of the Bishop of Rome."

For this reason it would seem that the period in which John Paul II was dying – late March, early April 2005 – became so extraordinary. Although it was predicted long before that the death of this Pope would cause a great stir, the scale, depth and intensity of the worldwide reaction were truly another surprise. It seemed as though time stood still, and all the eyes of the world turned to the Vatican. The never-ending procession of people stretching over days and nights, holding *Santo Subito* signs, walking by and paying their last respects to the Holy Father, as well as the wind closing the Book of the Gospels laying on the Pope's coffin all contributed to the image of the Polish Pope's pontificate being full of surprises.

The surprises didn't end once the Holy Father's body was placed in the grave at St. Peter's Basilica. It was expected that his beatification process might commence prior to the five-year waiting period required by Canon Law, yet the decision announced by Benedict XVI already on May 13, 2005, testified to a speeding up of the process (the actual decision carried the date of May 9, 2005 – barely a month after the funeral!).

At the same time, testimonies about healings and other graces attributed to the prayerful intervention of John Paul II began to arrive from around the world.

These were like echoes of the many *Santo Subito* calls heard at St. Peter's Square on the day of the funeral.

*he universe in which man lives is not limited to the order that can be ascertained through logic or the senses. A miracle is a "sign" that the order we perceive is superseded by a "Power from above", and that it is therefore subjected to it. This "Power from above" (Luke 24:49), in other words God Himself, is above the natural order. He controls it, but also lets us see both through it and outside of it that man's destiny is God's kingdom.*

John Paul II
"Miracles Manifest the Supernatural Order"
General Audience, January 13, 1988

# AN AVALANCHE OF MIRACLES

On July 1, 2004, John Paul II received sixteen-year-old Rafał of Lubaczów in private audience. The boy had lymphoma. A few months after the audience, Rafał was healed of the disease.

Immediately after the Holy Father's funeral, Piotr Piwowarczyk, chairman of the *Mam marzenie* (I Have a Dream) Foundation, which fulfills the wishes of seriously ill children, told the Polish Press Agency the story of Rafał and that Rafał had asked him to arrange the private audience with the Pope.

"It seemed nearly impossible, even when Rafał, his parents and siblings were already in Rome, that he would meet the Holy Father," recalled Piwowarczyk. "Despite earlier assurances that Rafał would meet the Holy Father, it suddenly appeared that there would be no chance for the meeting. He was not even allowed to give the Holy Father a letter written by other children suffering from cancer in Cracow. As he packed his belongings in disappointment and set out for the airport with his family, I called Archbishop Dziwisz and asked for his help, recounting to him Rafał's story. The Papal Secretary told me that Rafał and his family should come to the Vatican. The private audience was held on the first of July and lasted a few minutes. Rafał never revealed what he spoke about with Pope John Paul II."

The director of the foundation did not provide personal details on Rafal but did say that the disease went into remission and Rafał attributes it to John Paul II.

On September 14, 2003, John Paul II celebrated Mass in Bratislava, concluding a three-day visit in Slovakia. Among the people who received Communion from the hands of the Pope was a twelve-year-old girl. Her father, Tibor Uljacki, told the Polish Catholic news agency KAI that in the previous year during a papal audience in Rome he had asked the Holy Father to pray for his daughter who was ill with leukemia. After some time, the child was made well. "Now, the Holy Father wanted to meet her in person," said the young man. "When I shared this happy news with Archbishop Henryk Nowacki, the Papal Nuncio in Slovakia, he told me with full conviction that we are talking about a miraculous healing."

 In June 2002, an Italian boy took part in a private Mass celebrated by the Holy Father in his private chapel. The boy had a poor immune system; he had earlier been treated in the hospital for inflammation of the kidneys and intestines, as well as bronchitis. As OZON magazine reported, John Paul II briefly spoke with the boy and stroked him on the cheek. The child felt a sensation of warmth. Later on, it was revealed that the boy had been completely cured. *"Holy Father, thank you for giving me the chance to meet a saint,"* he wrote, in gratitude for his healing. The boy added that he prayed the rosary each day for the health of John Paul II. The Holy Father wrote back, *"Let us thank God. The Lord is good!"*

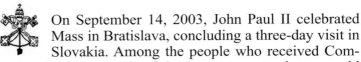 Sixteen-year-old Angela Baronni met with John Paul II during the World Youth Days in Toronto in 2002. Angela was ill with bone marrow cancer. The Holy Father prayed over her, put his hands on her head and made the sign of the cross. Soon after, Angela began to get well. She got out of her wheelchair and her doctor ascertained that she had indeed been cured. When the Holy Father died, she was studying at university in Toronto. Angela's story made it onto television in Canada not long after. In the program, Angela showed pictures of herself with the

Holy Father and told her story. Her doctor commented that Angela's cure was something he could not explain. "Can you tell us what the Pope said to you?" asked the TV host. "Yes," she answered, "it's not a secret anymore. He just said a few words; namely that the Lord Jesus loves me greatly and wants me to be healthy. I believed the Holy Father and I know that it was he who intervened for me in asking for health from Jesus – and that's why he will always stay here in my heart."

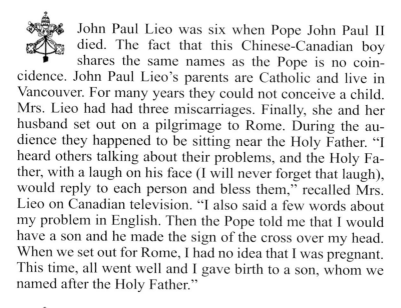 John Paul Lieo was six when Pope John Paul II died. The fact that this Chinese-Canadian boy shares the same names as the Pope is no coincidence. John Paul Lieo's parents are Catholic and live in Vancouver. For many years they could not conceive a child. Mrs. Lieo had had three miscarriages. Finally, she and her husband set out on a pilgrimage to Rome. During the audience they happened to be sitting near the Holy Father. "I heard others talking about their problems, and the Holy Father, with a laugh on his face (I will never forget that laugh), would reply to each person and bless them," recalled Mrs. Lieo on Canadian television. "I also said a few words about my problem in English. Then the Pope told me that I would have a son and he made the sign of the cross over my head. When we set out for Rome, I had no idea that I was pregnant. This time, all went well and I gave birth to a son, whom we named after the Holy Father."

In 1999, John Paul II was in Poland on his seventh papal pilgrimage. On Sunday, June 13, he led the Liturgy of the Word in front of the Cathedral of St. Michael the Archangel and St. Florian the Martyr in Warsaw. "Two children greeted the Holy Father at that time," recalled Fr. Henryk Zielinski, who was in charge of the local edition of *Niedziela* magazine. "One of the children was five-year-old Peter. Two years earlier, the boy had fallen ill; the doctors found that he had a malignant brain tumour. The situation was deemed hopeless. It was then that his mother and grandmother decided to write to the Pope with the request that he pray to God that Peter might be healed. Some time later a reply came from the Vatican confirming that the Holy Father was praying for the child. Soon after, the boy felt better - and tomograms indicated that the tumour was gone."

 Twenty-nine-year old Emil Barbar of Australia was born with cerebral palsy. Doctors told his parents that he would always need a wheelchair. As he grew older, it was found that Emil mumbled and could not speak in clear phrases. In 1980, his mother Rosemary took him to Rome. On Easter Monday, they gathered together with a group of disabled people at St. Peter's Square. Seeing John Paul II, Emil began to shout: "Holy Father, come this way! Come this way!" The Pope gave him a kiss on the head. His mother began to cry. The Holy Father asked her, "Why are you crying?" "My son can't walk," she said. "Take him to Lourdes," was the reply. "You will see that he will walk." The Pope handed her a cross and rosary. Rosemary and Emil travelled to the French shrine. There, she immersed Emil in the pool that formed following a Marian apparition. "Mother, don't cry – the Mother of God told me that I will walk," said Emil. They returned to Australia. Emil continued to attend school for the disabled. Six weeks later, he stood up and got out of his wheelchair. He was healed. A quarter-century after this event, Emil is a graduate of law school and wishes to become a lawyer.

 Archbishop Stanisław Dziwisz, who served as personal secretary to Pope John Paul II, told Polish journalist Krzysztof Tadej that at one time a telegram was received at the Vatican from the parents of a very ill child in Great Britain. According to the *Santo Subito* publication, the Pope prayed for the child in his chapel. The boy was healed at precisely that moment in which John Paul II prayed for him. The same issue of *Santo Subito* carried the story of Mariusz Drapikowski, a well-known artisan working with amber in Gdańsk. In 2002, he began to experience the first symptoms of multiple sclerosis. The following year he lost strength in his legs, then in his arms and began to lose his vision. Toward the end of 2003, he travelled to Rome to attend a private audience with John Paul II. The Prior of Jasna Góra, present as well, said that he would like the artist to make a dress out of amber for the portrait of Our Lady of Jasna Góra. Upon his return to Poland, Drapikowski's illness receded. On August 26, 2005, Archbishop Stanisław Dziwisz blessed the finished dress at Jasna Góra. Drapikowski then presented his testimony: "When, thanks to the Paulines of Jasna Góra, I managed to get a private audience with the Holy Father John Paul II in December 2003, and when the Holy Father blessed me and placed his palm on my head, I felt that I became filled with new, unfamiliar strength. The following months brought an improvement in my state of health. I believe, Our Lady of Jasna Góra, that through the intervention of the Holy Father you gave sight back to my eyes and strength back to my legs."

Following the death of John Paul II, the Italian press recalled a story from three years earlier, told by Archbishop Stanisław Dziwisz to Italian journalists Andrei Tornelli of *Il Giornale* and Marco Tossati of *La Stampa*. The occurrence took place in 1998. An acquaintance of the papal secretary turned to him on behalf of a wealthy American friend who was suffering from a brain tumour. The friend had three wishes: to see the Pope, to travel to Jerusalem and to return to the United States where he wished to die. This person attended the Papal Mass at Castel Gandolfo and received Communion from the Holy Father. Archbishop Dziwisz later found out that this man was not even a Christian but a Jew – after which he told his acquaintance that non-Catholics cannot receive Communion. A few weeks later the acquaintance called the Papal Secretary to tell him that his friend's tumour was gone.

In his book, *Farewell – Till We Meet in Paradise*, Arturo Mari recalls his wife's sister, who developed cancer. According to the doctors, she had at most a month to live. Mari's wife, who went to Ecuador to be with her dying sibling, had asked her husband for some item belonging to the Pope and got a rosary and handkerchief. Mari advised his wife to apply the handkerchief close to her sister's cancer and to pray the rosary. The illness went into remission thereafter.

Cardinal Francesco Marchisano, archpresbyter of St. Peter's Basilica, testified that he once lost his voice as a result of surgery only to gain it back, as he believed, through the intercession of John Paul II. The Cardinal was celebrating the second of nine Masses (called the "novendiali") traditionally done following the burial of Popes. "Five years ago, I underwent an operation on an artery in my neck," recalled Marchisano during his homily on April 9, 2005, at St. Peter's Basilica. "After coming out of anesthesia, I found that I had somehow lost my voice. It was due to an error by the surgeon. A few days later the Holy Father invited me to lunch. He listened attentively while I tried with difficulty to speak. Finally, he got up. He came over to me and touched the spot where I had been operated on and said, "Don't worry; you'll be well soon. God will help you to speak once again." I was very moved ... I hugged him like one hugs one's father. He, too, was moved and said "Thank you". Following this meeting, the Cardinal underwent therapy and regained his voice. When asked if he thought this was a miracle, the Cardinal answered, "Possibly. Saints have power."

 Marek Skwarnicki, poet, writer, and friend of John Paul II, recalls that in 1987 while in Rome he fell gravely ill with a heart ailment. In his book *I Greet and Bless You*, Skwarnicki wrote: "I know from those present at the Papal dinner on the day of my coronary diagnosis at Ospedale Aurelia that when the Holy Father was informed of my near-critical state he got up and went to the chapel to pray. In all likelihood, it is thanks to his intervention that I lived through it." Twenty-four hours later, he underwent a bypass and the crisis was no more. Fifteen years later, Skwarnicki was diagnosed with cancer of the large intestine and underwent an operation. "Today I believe that it was again thanks to the prayers of John Paul II that my life was saved,"

wrote Skwarnicki. "The doctors continue to be amazed by the absence of metastases, because the disease was already advanced by the time of the operation."

In 1979 during the Holy Father's visit to Ireland, Bernhard and Mary Mulligan presented their daughter to him. She had a kidney disease and doctors felt that she would die within a few months. The parents waited in the crowd, and, seeing the Holy Father passing by, they showed him their little girl. He came over, paused, and touched the ailing girl gently. A short time afterwards, the child became healthy.

In an interview for Italian television's Canale 5, Papal Secretary Archbishop Stanislaw Dziwisz revealed that he did not keep records of these occurrences. "I can only say that the Holy Father did not want to hear about it and always said, 'God performs miracles, I simply pray. Those are divine mysteries. Let's not dwell on it.'"

# Chapter 2.

## SIGNS FROM GOD

*M*iracles are not opposed to the forces and laws of nature. They merely imply a certain empirical suspension of their ordinary function and not their annulment. Indeed, the miracles described in the Gospel indicate the existence of a Power superior to the forces and laws of nature, but which at the same time operates according to the demands of nature itself, even though surpassing its actual normal capacity. Is not this what happens, for example, in every miraculous cure?

John Paul II
"Miracles Manifest the Supernatural Order"
General Audience, January 13, 1988

# ANNUNTIO VOBIS GAUDIUM MAGNUM

*"I announce to you a great joy."*

Kay Kelly watched the TV screen incredulously and listened to the speaker translating into English these Latin words: *"Annuntio vobis gaudium magnum. Habemus Papam. Eminentissimum ac Reverentissimum Dominum, Dominum Carolum Sancte Romanae Ecclesiae Cardinalem Wojtyła qui sibi nomen imposuit Ioannem Paulum Secundum…"*

Kay saw a cross appearing on the balcony of the Vatican Basilica and, immediately behind, the broad figure of a man on whose shoulders lay a large stole.

The speaker explained that the newly elected Pope was a Polish Cardinal and that the decision of the conclave came as a great surprise because for the first time in over four centuries a non-Italian was chosen to sit on the throne of St. Peter. What's more, it was someone from behind the Iron Curtain.

"Don't ask me how I knew, but I knew then that somehow this person would enter into my life," Kay told me 27 years after the fact.

At that time, Kay was in Clatterbridge Hospital in Liverpool, where she had been undergoing successive chemotherapy treatments. In March 1978, it was discovered that Kay had cancer. Malignant granuloma, also known as Hodgkin's dis-

23

ease, was the diagnosis. This didn't mean much to Kay, but the expression on the doctor's face clearly indicated that it was not good news. Later she found out that an especially dangerous growth had invaded her breast.

At the time of her diagnosis, Kay was 34 years old, married for fifteen years and mother of three children: fourteen-year-old David, thirteen-year-old Kevin and twelve-year-old Jacqueline. They lived in Liverpool, which is where Kay was born on June 29, 1944. She eagerly stresses that it is the same day on which the first Pope, St. Peter, and the greatest Apostle, St. Paul, are remembered. Her given name was Catherine, but later everyone would call her Kay and the name stuck (she herself, though, had always preferred to be called by her given name).

She was the daughter of a mariner and a housewife. Kay's father worked aboard ocean freightliners in the North Atlantic, even during World War II while German U-boats were attacking Allied convoys. Three years after Kay was born, her parents separated. When she turned 15, Kay quit school and went to work. When her mother began to run a bar, Kay quit work and began helping at home, since she had many siblings.

"That's when the thing that had to happen did happen," she recalled. One evening as I was helping my mom at the bar, Pat Kelly, a tall docker, came in for a drink. It was as if we ran into each other and it was love at first sight! As usual, the predictable choir of voices emerged saying that it wouldn't last, that we would regret it, all the usual stuff that people say to dissuade you."

Four months later they got married. Kay Peeney became a housewife, Mrs. Kelly. She dreamed of starting a family and therefore felt that she should stay at home.

"My kids know where to find me when they need me," she said. "I'm at home waiting for them."

She lived this way for fifteen years.

"You're wearing yourself out," her friends and family would tell her.

Kay Kelly of Liverpool, England, suffering from cancer,
attends a Papal audience with Pope John Paul II.
March 14, 1979.

"No, I am just slimming down," she would reply, believing that she was getting thinner because she was trying to. She attributed the pain in her chest to physical work. In the end, though, she agreed to get a check-up. She found out that she had cancer.

Kay ended up at Clatterbridge hospital in Liverpool, which specialized in oncology. Following her first round of treatments, she returned home. Three months later the chest pains returned.

"I had ten rounds of treatments at Clatterbridge," recalled Kay. "Following radiotherapy I lost my hair and developed other unpleasant side-effects and finally metastases. Chemotherapy was my last hope."

Her talk with the doctor was short and straightforward.

"Please tell me about my condition," asked Kay.

"You know, the disease is very serious," began the doctor somewhat uneasily.

"How much time do I have left?"

"It's odd to hear a woman asking that – usually men ask me that question. Well, if you can finish your chemo, maybe a year or two."

Kay was dumbfounded since she actually felt fine, but she knew that things could change quickly.

"I know you asked for money, Doctor. I'll do everything I can," she finally said.

Kay's physician, Dr. Derek Edwards, had been fundraising for a few months to establish laboratories at the hospital where new treatments for cancer could be found. Kay decided to take part in the initiative.

She wasn't entirely sure what to do. After she started chemotherapy, her body became so weak that she had difficulty moving about.

"I got two Easter eggs from the store at the corner as a reward," she recalled. "My children distributed lottery tickets among their neighbours and we managed to raise 14 pounds. That's how it started."

During that time, the closure of the radiation treatment facility where Kay was receiving radiotherapy was announced. She decided to protest the closure by attending the municipal council meeting with signs she had prepared the night before. "The Liverpool clinic must stay open. Cancer patients are suffering enough already. Give us research laboratories in Clatterbridge," she wrote. Kay stood at the rear during the council meeting with her signs in hand and listened to the proceedings.

"The council members were allocating monies for all sorts of things," she recalled.

"As usual, nobody wanted to listen. I thought about all the children undergoing radiotherapy. I raised my sign up higher. I felt as though everything in me was boiling over. The council meeting moved forward, and I was preparing myself for action. Finally I couldn't take it anymore. I took the sign, ran across the hall and laid it right in front of the chairman, Sir Kenneth Thompson.

Voices stirred in the hall. The council members began to yell: "Get her out of here!"

And they did. The story made it to the press. The next day, Sir Kenneth invited Kay "for a cup of tea". He wanted to know what it was all about. Kay told him. A great fundraising drive began, which eventually brought in a million pounds.

During the fundraising, Kay met with many famous personalities: Muhammad Ali and then Prime Minister Jim Callaghan, to name two. She was even given the title of *British Catholic of the Year.*

All this, however, failed to change a major consideration – her illness was not letting up but appeared to be advancing all the more.

"I prayed to God to give me strength to accept the inevitable," Kay said. "I knew other women who had mastectomies and yet they were somehow able to keep smiling. I saw dying men who were still able to smile. I prayed for my children then as well, feeling it to be altogether possible that they might be angry at God and rebel against Him for what was happening to me, and I wanted to avoid this. I wanted them to know Christ and to know that they were loved. I prayed to the Blessed Virgin asking her for time. I needed time."

During this time, Kay learned of a woman who had succumbed to cancer in Manchester and who had managed to raise a large sum of money for the hospital in which she was receiving treatment. The woman's name was Pat Seed. Was the example of this woman to foretell what awaited Kay? Everything seemed to indicate precisely that.


On March 11, 1979, having left the hospital, Kay knelt in front of the statue of Mary in her local parish. She prayed while looking at the figure. As she knelt, she felt a deep sense of uneasiness but all of a sudden she became quieted. She doesn't know where it came from, but she felt a strong conviction that she need no longer fear the disease that was threatening her life. Moreover, she couldn't understand why she had the firm conviction that she would meet the Pope.

"How are you, Kay?" asked the pastor, walking by. "What are you planning in the near future?"

"Soon I will meet the Pope," she answered.

The pastor looked at Kay with empathy. He figured that her illness must be making her delusional. *To meet with John Paul II?* True, the pastor knew that this new Pope from Poland was conducting his papal ministry in an entirely different way from his predecessors. Even so, it couldn't mean that he saw ordinary people, no matter that they be gravely ill. Kings and queens, heads of state, important people – these could surely get a visit with the Pope. But others?

Upon returning home, Kay also wondered if she hadn't fallen victim to some kind of illusion. What reason, after all, would she have to meet the Pope? He had just been elected five months earlier so he surely had a million other matters more

Kay Kelly with boxer Muhammad Ali (Cassius Clay)
during her fundraising drive for the Clatterbridge
oncological hospital.

important to deal with than to raise the spirits of an English-woman whom he didn't even know.

A phone call soon cast aside those doubts. A representative of the Knights of Columbus called Kay and informed her of a prize awarded her by this well-known Catholic charity. The Knights had decided to honour Kay's efforts during her fundraiser to help those suffering with cancer. The prize consisted of exactly two airline tickets to Rome for immediate use.

The next day, Kay and her son David were aboard an aircraft flying from Liverpool to Rome. Prior to departure, Kay learned that the Archbishop of Liverpool, Derek Worlock, arranged a semi-private audience with the Pope for her immediately following the Wednesday General Audience on March 14.

They arrived in Rome at night on March 13. Their flight was delayed and they arrived in the Eternal City at three o'clock in the morning. In the afternoon they went to St. Peter's Square and later for tea (traditionally held at five o'clock) to the seminary for priests who could not study in Great Britain after King Henry VIII made Catholicism illegal there. In the evening, Kay set out for Piazza Navona and was enthralled by Bernini's fountain with its four sculpted figures representing the Nile River, the Danube River, the Ganges River and La Plata.

The following day, a cleric from the English seminary came to the hotel to pick them up and take them to the Vatican.

"At the time, I wasn't sure what our meeting with the Holy Father was going to be like," recalled David Lowis. "The rector of the seminary only told me that he hoped that the Holy Father would be able to meet with Kay."

They got to the gate leading to the small square on the left side of St. Peter's Basilica. This was the entrance to the Paul VI Auditorium, which was designed by well-known Italian architect Pier Luigi Nervi.

"At 12:15, the Holy Father began to cross the auditorium. Camera lights flashed all around him. People stretched out their hands," recalled the seminarian. "The Holy Father's walk through the auditorium took him about half-an-hour. I saw Kay sitting patiently in the section devoted to the sick. The Holy Father then began his address in Italian. I translated for Kay and David. Then the Holy Father spoke in French, English, German and Spanish, to invite everyone to sing the Our Father.

"The audience was nearing its end. The Pope left the podium and made his way to greet the sick. David Lowis noted that the John Paul II was coming in their direction – and was soon right in front of them!"

"Your Holiness, may I introduce Mrs. Kay Kelly to you?" asked the cleric.

"Oh, Mrs. Kelly from Liverpool," replied the Pope in English.

"I've heard a lot about you."

They spoke for a moment. The Holy Father signed his autograph on a photo of himself which Kay had brought, dedicating it to her son, David. Then he hugged Kay. The Holy Father moved on, but suddenly turned around and approached Kay again.

"I am very proud of you. You are an excellent mother," said the Holy Father, and then he moved on.

What was it like for Kay to meet Pope John Paul II?

"It takes a lot of courage to be that human, and it seems to me that he had that gift," recalled Kay. "I felt that my meeting with the Pope was the turning point in my illness. His love and understanding created an atmosphere of joy that enveloped everyone and everything in his midst. His interior peace and self control were manifested in his smile. It was very easy to speak with him. I was also struck by the fact that he didn't seem burdened by protocol. This Pope showed that he was a Shepherd of the people. I remember telling him how I hoped that one day he would visit Liverpool."

Kay's stay in Rome lasted less than 20 hours. Following the audience, Kay returned home.

On a subsequent visit to the hospital, the doctors examining Kay were completely shocked to find that there was absolutely no cancer in her system! They could find no signs of the first bout of the disease, nor any signs of the metastases that had developed. The story spread quickly and news of the healing reached the Vatican. At the first opportunity, journalists asked Pope John Paul II about the extraordinary healing.

"Her faith has cured her," was the Holy Father's explanation.

*"Her faith has cured her."* Kay recalls the Holy Father's words 26 years later. I hear the voice of an older woman through the telephone receiver. She has gained in years, of course, but she still has the same fighting spirit today that she had back then, when nobody believed she had a chance to survive.

"It happened some time ago," Kay says, "and in all the years since then I have tried to serve God."

How? Kay raised tens of thousands of pounds in support of the work of Mother Teresa, who opened a small convent for the Missionaries of Charity in Liverpool. She also spent time with those dying individuals who had asked for her to be with them in their final moments.

"I prayed for them believing that life does not end but that there is only eternal love when one goes to be with God," said Kay. "I also sent two young people to see the Pope. Both were sick with cancer and both had abandoned their faith. Before their deaths, both regained their faith. That is a true miracle. People say to me, 'Kay, you were healed – that's a miracle,' to which I say 'the miracle happens when you change your life.' One of the young people was a woman named Julia; she was married and had children. The other was a handsome mulatto boy from southern Liverpool. Neither of them ever thought they'd see the Holy Father. I was at

"I am very proud of you. You are an excellent mother."
- Pope John Paul II speaking to Kay Kelly at the Vatican,
March 14, 1979.

their funerals. I wasn't sad though, because I knew that they had died in peace."

And Kay, how is she doing over a quarter-century later?

In 2004, Kay's husband passed away from cancer. That year she also learned that she had been a mother not of three but four children.

"When I was sick, I was told that I had to undergo a hysterectomy. At first I didn't agree because I wanted to have more children. Then the doctors persisted in order to change my mind. I thought I was pregnant at the time, so I refused. But they kept convincing me that it was all in my head. In the end they did the hysterectomy. Last year I ordered copies of my hospital papers and inadvertently learned that I had been right – I *was* pregnant at the time. I don't know if it was a girl or a boy. I call the unborn child Michael. I later visited the doctor who was treating me back then and asked him, "Why did you do that?" "It was a long time ago," he retorted. "We weren't obliged to tell you."

In the spring of 2005, Kay listened with anguish to the news coming out of the Vatican.

"I was very sad upon learning of the Holy Father's death. But I know that he went straight to heaven. Yes, I continue to pray to him," she added. "This prayer gives me strength, hope and gives meaning to my life. We need prayer and people like the Holy Father who will intercede for us so that we can do good. I expect that he will be beatified."

Kay admits that while she always had faith, in her youth she used to criticize the popes.

"I couldn't understand why they were so inaccessible and kept apart from the people," she said. "The Holy Father is supposed to be a Father figure – yet I didn't feel that to be the case at all. John Paul II changed all that; he went out among the faithful. He even met with me, a simple housewife from Liverpool."

Kay would like to visit the homeland of John Paul II. She has a reason:

"I'd like to bring some of your priests to England," she said. "We need them immensely - there is a shortage of priests here."

In 2000, Kay began the second battle of her life: she fought to re-open the famous church in Liverpool dedicated to the Virgin Mary, Mother of Angels. One of the reasons it had been closed was the lack of priests in the diocese. Kay Kelly believes that the presence of priests from Poland, with their deep spiritual life, could turn the situation around.

One question remained: What did she feel when she learned that her days were numbered?

"It's strange, but in those months which I thought were going to be my last, I was full of happiness. I felt that I could help others and that, thanks to this, I was pleasing to God. Every second, every minute and every day I was aware of what a precious gift life is. Living every moment in happiness gives a feeling of being fully alive."

Was she scared? Did she rebel against what had befallen her?

"Sometimes people ask, 'Why me? Why did this have to happen to me?' Christ never asked 'why me' – He persevered until the end. The reward comes when one accepts one's situation. If you pray 'Your will be done' and you believe in prayer, miracles happen. They happen when you stop asking 'why me?' and you accept everything with gratitude, as a gift. We have to avoid fear because fear can destroy everything. I know it well. I understand those who say, 'I could take a pill and it'd be all over with'. I sympathize with those who have little faith. Fear always lurks behind. Fear comes from Satan; he is the one fomenting your fear. Fear can be defeated by praying: 'I believe in God; may His will be done.' Fear is worst of all. You can get by with the illness but fear is much more powerful because it destroys your perception of reality. When we are afraid, we wish to turn around. But when we surrender, God steps forth. And and if we trust in Him, we regain our strength."

How did Kay feel being at the edge of death?

"Imminent death sharpens perception. Now I must use that sharpened perception to help others. I know that I must speak to the ill, especially those who have cancer. That helps them. People call me and are glad when they know that I'm coming. I tell them to thank God for all the good they've received in their lives. Yes, it's important to be able to accept one's illness. I know how hard that is, but I tell them that they will be much happier once they offer their pain to God. Don't expect rewards now. Don't expect anything. Just accept that which must be accepted. Therein lies the mystery."

*The soteriological order is rooted in the Incarnation. The "miracles-signs" of which the Gospels speak also have their foundation in the same reality of the God-Man. This reality-mystery embraces and surpasses all the miraculous happenings connected with Christ's messianic mission. It may be said that the Incarnation is the "miracle of miracles," the radical and permanent "miracle" of the new order of creation.*

John Paul II
"Miracles Manifest the Supernatural Order"
General Audience, January 13, 1988

# VICTORIA
# MEANS
# VICTORY

*The year 1981*

That evening, his worst fears were confirmed. For some time he had felt that the coming months would bring bad news, but he hoped that the time hadn't yet come. Word got to him that something was about to happen, so he spent the nights away from home. Going to sleep on December 12, he had no idea that he'd wake up in a different country.

On Monday, December 14, Franciszek Szechyński was about to begin working for the Solidarity movement in Poland's Lower Śląsk region. But martial law had been declared in Poland that weekend. The communist authorities were arresting members of Solidarity all across the country. Thousands were held in detention.

Franciszek was living with his family in Wałbrzych. Feeling that something was about to happen, he stayed away from home for a few weeks, not wanting to put his wife Danuta and their three children at risk. But following the imposition of martial law, Franciszek's attempts didn't make much of a difference in any case. "Your father is acting against the state," the school personnel would tell the young Szechyński children. Franciszek's wife was often approached by state security personnel. Franciszek went into hiding for a while but then decided to come out when he heard that lower- and middle-rank Solidarity members were being let out of detention. What he heard from the state police left him with no doubts.

"You have nothing to go back to in Lower Śląsk," a state security official told him. "And be careful that something doesn't happen to you."

Franciszek worried for his wife and children – especially after Danuta learned that she was expecting their fourth child. They decided to leave for Warsaw, knowing that they could count on the help of friends involved in the Solidarity movement. They had no clue that months of difficulty lay ahead. Again, it turned out that they couldn't all live together. Danuta and the children stayed at one family's home while Franciszek had to stay with another family. They prepared for the birth of their child with some difficulty, as no Warsaw hospital would formally take them. Fortunately, there was no shortage of well-meaning people, both among the doctors and the nurses. Someone from the emergency department told them that when Danuta goes into labour, they would have to call for an ambulance. It was arranged that the ambulance would take her to the hospital, where the staff would be informed of everything in advance. They would treat the case as unexpected and take her in, later signing her out before anyone would notice that she had no official right to hospital care.

"You know, we could just emigrate," Franciszek said to Danuta one October afternoon as they went for a walk through the Łazienki Park in Warsaw. Danuta was about a month away from giving birth, as was plainly visible.

"Emigrate? And be without a home again?"

"They're giving away passports to those associated with Solidarity. I'm certain we could get them without any problems."

"But what do you mean? Those would be one-way passports. They'd never let us back in to the country."

"But what's holding us here? We're staying with others without a place of our own and we can't even live together as one family. What future is there for us here?"

Danuta had the same thoughts deep inside, but she was afraid of the changes that such a prospect offered – a new and unknown country, an unknown language. How would the children adapt to life in a new land? They had already been through so much, first in Wałbrzych and now here. On the other hand, Danuta had fears about staying in Poland just the same – she had enough of the constant surveillance and was worried for Franciszek as well. She didn't want to think of anything happening to him.

"In any case, the child will be born here in Poland, and later we'll see."

"What'll we name him?"

"If it's a girl, then obviously Victoria."


They could still spend Independence Day (unofficially November 11th then) together. In the evening, Danuta felt contractions coming on. Keeping in mind their plan, they called for the ambulance, which came unexpectedly quickly. Danuta was on her way to the hospital. For Franciszek, it was a long night. Finally he saw the doctor in the hospital hallway.

"Congratulations, you have a daughter," Franciszek heard.

"Is everything okay? How's my wife feeling?"

"Your wife's doing well, but the little girl was born with a growth in the vicinity of her heart. It would be best if you took her to the Children's Health Centre. I can't keep them here beyond tomorrow morning anyway."

They had been forewarned that they'd have to leave the hospital quickly following the birth of the child since they were there illegally. News that the child had a growth, however, was a total shock to Franciszek. As if they had not suffered enough over the past months ...

"There's a really good doctor at the Children's Health Centre who knows how to get things done," winked the doctor sympathetically. "She can help you."

The following days did not bring good news; the growth was getting bigger. And the doctor to whom they had been referred threw her hands up in desperation, saying, "We can't help her here. You might have a better chance abroad."

Again, the chance of emigrating surfaced.

"Where could they treat her?" they asked. "We can try to emigrate to the United States."

"I'd suggest Canada instead," said the doctor. "There is an excellent children's hospital in Toronto where they specialize in treating these kinds of problems."

Franciszek went to the state security office.

"I wish to emigrate from Poland with my family."

The officials promised to have passports ready in a few days. They also got airline tickets without difficulty. First they would travel from Warsaw to London and then across the Atlantic to Toronto. They were not leaving blindly; they knew that there were campaigns under way to assist political refugees from Poland. Toronto's Archbishop, Cardinal Gerald Emmett Carter, was also involved. Carter had turned to each parish in the archdiocese asking that it take one Polish family under its care. The Szechyński family was assisted by St. John's Parish. They could finally live together as a family unit. They received material assistance and help in finding work. Most importantly, however, they could get Victoria to the hospital immediately.

When they arrived for the first time, they could not believe that a hospital could look so clean and bright with such wide corridors and tidy rooms. The nurses and doctors spoke to them pleasantly and with a smile. None of this changed the fact that Victoria's growth was getting larger, and the doctors didn't seem able to propose an effective course of treatment.

"Only an operation might help, but with the child being in this condition and at such a young age, she might not make it," the parents were told. "The risk is very high."

"And if she doesn't have the operation?"

"Then she has at most three more years to live," said the doctor.

Over a year and a half had passed when Danuta and Franciszek learned that Pope John Paul II would be visiting Canada. The Pope would come to Toronto and meet with its large Polish community. They tried to get seats in the first row. To their pleasant surprise, Danuta and Franciszek learned that after the meeting the Holy Father would bless the sick, including Victoria.

## IT WAS THEIR GREAT HOPE THAT JOHN PAUL II WOULD BLESS THEIR DAUGHTER

Were they counting on a miracle?

They wanted him to touch her. They weren't counting on anything, but they knew that it would bring them inner peace to know that the Holy Father had blessed Victoria. They wanted to put Victoria in God's hands, but they wanted to ensure that God's blessing would be with Victoria.

In the late afternoon on September 14, 1984, they took their seats at Exhibition Place in Toronto. This was the last event on the itinerary for the Pope's visit to Canada on that day. The Pope was to arrive after 8 o'clock in the evening. They were elated to see the pope-mobile arriving at the stadium a half-hour early.

The atmosphere was enlivened by the crowd of 60,000 Canadian Poles who were enthusiastically welcoming John Paul II.

"For a number of days now, I have been travelling between the cities of this country and have seen many signs bearing the name Solidarity," said the Holy Father.

It was the first time that they heard the Pope actually say the word Solidarity. How clearly they suddenly recalled those days in Poland – Danuta's pregnancy, the many months spent staying with others in Warsaw, all the nerves and anguish, Danuta's giving birth to Victoria, Victoria's illness and their emigrating to Canada. They knew John Paul II to be an ardent supporter of the movement for change, which had been launched in August 1980. Now they were convinced that it was so. The Pope spoke about World War II and the Universal Declaration of Human Rights. He now said he wanted to explain what the signs bearing Solidarity all across Canada meant to him.

"My dear Brothers and Sisters, my dear fellow Poles! It means that over the last forty years – but especially in the 1980s – the Polish nation managed to write a chapter born of the same ideals as the Universal Declaration of Human Rights. The word 'Solidarity' reflects that same order, where the human being is placed at the centre. The dignity and rights of man are the criteria around which work, culture, social life and national life must be established. For this reason we pay respect to 'Solidarity' as a word, a symbol and a reality. I think that for our nation, which in recent times has had to tread a difficult path, this word harkens back to a similar striving born of parallel circumstances and having the same ends which are at the source of the struggle for freedom. We want to be ourselves and to live our lives."

That same day marked the Feast of the Holy Cross, and the Holy Father remarked in his address:

"It's a question of man not being trampled by the world - but that he may have eternal life in God. That is the meaning of the Cross."

A few moments later he concluded:

"Dear Brothers and Sisters, the Cross is a sign of our faith, our hope and our love. Let us bring our heartfelt prayers to the foot of the Cross, trusting that they will be heard."

Danuta, Franciszek and Victoria waited impatiently for the moment when John Paul II would arrive at their section. The ceremony was nearing its end. At a certain moment they noticed men in suits with earphones approaching the stage where the Holy Father and his entourage were. The men exchanged some words with the organizers. The Szechyńskis didn't think anything of it at first, but later when the Holy Father did not come to greet the sick, it appeared that the meeting had been cut short by security officials. Why, they wondered … had there been a threat of attack or some other danger? They never did find out. One thing was certain: Victoria did not receive a personal Papal blessing from John Paul II during his first visit to Canadian soil.

## THEY DID NOT GIVE UP

The Szechyńskis completely rejected the option of an operation for Victoria; too many specialists had said that the little girl would not survive one. They thought that if she was to die, that she should be with her parents. They would pray, believing that prayer was in fact Victoria's only hope.

Nor did they give up on meeting with the Pope – if it didn't work out in Toronto, then maybe it would in Rome. They wrote to the Vatican. Would John Paul II have the time, though, to meet with some unknown Poles who had emigrated to Canada? And even if so, how long would they have to wait to get such a meeting? They knew that dignitaries and others had their timetables set many months in advance, yet here the time that doctors gave Victoria to live was getting ever shorter. The growth had reached such a size that it occupied nearly half her tiny body. It looked terrible, yet it was even harder to look into Victoria's eyes; there was so much sadness in them that it was heart wrenching.

Three weeks later, an invitation arrived from the Vatican.

Danuta took Victoria to Rome, while Franciszek stayed in Toronto with the rest of the children.

It was March 1985.

As long as she lives, Danuta will never forget the meeting or conversation with John Paul II. A few seconds after the audience began, she felt as though she was about to meet with the

Father who is theirs alone. The Pope took little Victoria in his hands and kissed her.

"Trust in God," the Holy Father said. "If He decides that He wants to have her with Him, He will take her. If he wants her to remain with you, you don't have to worry or do anything at all. Treat her the same as your other children. God will decide the outcome."

Victoria looked at the Pope the whole time as if in a trance. Danuta felt as though the child had relaxed. Little Victoria eagerly embraced the Holy Father and kissed him.

Danuta offered the Pope a tablecloth made by women who were imprisoned following the declaration of martial law in Poland. They spoke for a while about Poland and *Solidarity*. The next day, Danuta received pictures from the meeting with the Holy Father, pictures that became family relics.

Danuta and Victoria returned to Canada a week later. From the airport they went home. But they did not stay there for long.

"Franek, look, she's got a terrible fever," observed Danuta the same day. They didn't even bother to take Victoria's temperature since not only was it obvious that she had a fever, but she was literally hot to the touch. Her body even began to take on all sorts of colours.

"We're going to the hospital!" Franciszek decided.

Half an hour later, they entered the already familiar hospital building.

The next day did not bring good news. The doctors could not lessen the fever; Victoria was fading before them.

"She doesn't have much time left," said one doctor. "You can leave her here, if you wish ..."

They did not want to leave her. They took her, resigned to what was about to happen. They knew that it had to happen sooner or later. And at least she managed to get the Pope's blessing in time.

A few days passed. The girl was still alive and did not feel

Danuta Szechyński with her daughter Victoria in audience
with John Paul II, March 1985.

From left to right: Franciszek Szechyński; Danuta and Victoria
Szechynska; Victoria's fiancé Pawel Gogol.

any worse. On the contrary … one day she got up and asked to have something to eat, then ran – not walked, but ran – to the next room. They could not explain what had happened. So again, Danuta and Franciszek took Victoria to the hospital.

The doctor rubbed his eyes in amazement, looking at the growth which had amazingly become very small. Tests revealed that the illness had receded. It took two procedures to remove the remaining tissue, which proved to be no longer malignant. The Szechyńskis felt as though their daughter had been born anew. Now they didn't hesitate to look into her eyes; her sadness had disappeared and the little girl would even smile!

They took her regularly for follow-up tests. The results were always the same: Victoria had experienced a definitive cure. When she was twelve, a doctor told Victoria: "You certainly have a right to be grateful for what you and your mother believe in."

Although today Victoria is a healthy and athletic young woman, her mother still sometimes worries about her.

"If she feels worse or is tired, I worry and tell her to rest or to eat something."

To which Victoria answers: "Mom, don't worry. What will be will be. Things don't happen without a reason; everything has a meaning of some kind."

Every day Victoria makes the sign of the cross and says: "Thank You for giving me one more day, one more chance."


Victoria was twenty years old when John Paul II visited Toronto for World Youth Day 2002. On Sunday, July 28, 2002, she was among the throngs of people in Downsview Park, where the Pope was to celebrate the concluding Mass. Standing drenched by the rain that poured down prior to the beginning of the Mass, Victoria wondered why some of those around here were vacating the area. She, on the other hand, pushed forward to get as close as possible to the front and to John Paul II. She looked at his figure as the wind ruffled his liturgical vestments. On the Telebeam she could see his face which bore the signs of his struggle through illness. She listened as he spoke:

"Although I have lived through much darkness, under harsh totalitarian regimes, I have seen enough evidence to be unshakably convinced that no difficulty, no fear is so great that it can completely suffocate the hope that springs eternal in the hearts of the young!

"Do not let that hope die! Stake your lives on it! We are not the sum of our weaknesses and failures; we are the sum of the Father's love for us and our real capacity to become the image of his son, Jesus."

The Holy Father didn't know that among the few hundred thousand youths listening to him on that windy morning was the very same girl whom he blessed seventeen years earlier and who was cured of a life-threatening disease in a medically inexplicable way. "But I'm positive that he would recognize me right away if we were able to meet today," Victoria added.

Two and a half years later, Victoria sat in front of the television watching the news coming out of the Vatican. It was April 2, 2005. Nobody had any doubts that John Paul II was completing his earthly sojourn. Victoria knew that the previous day, upon hearing about the large presence of youth at St. Peter's Square, the Pope had whispered: "I looked for you, now you have come to me. And I thank you." She kept vigil, watching the images of St. Peter's Square now at dusk. At a certain moment she felt a desire to go to her room. She looked at the picture of the Pope with that little girl and her mother. It was a memento of that visit, exactly twenty years earlier. Victoria knelt down and began to pray. A few minutes later she heard that John Paul II had returned to the Heavenly Father's house.

*The potentiality of the forces of nature is actuated by divine intervention which extends this potential beyond the sphere of its normal capacity of action. This does not annul or frustrate the causality which God has communicated to created things, nor does it violate the natural laws established by God himself and inscribed in the structure of creation. But it exalts and in a certain way ennobles the capacity to operate or even to receive the effects of the operation of another, as happens precisely in the cures described by the Gospel.*

John Paul II
"Miracles Manifest the Supernatural Order"
General Audience, January 13, 1988

Five-year-old Heron Badillo, gravely ill with leukemia,
with his mother at the airport in Zacatecas, Mexico. May 12, 1990.

# TWO
# PHOTOGRAPHS

*Autumn 1990*

Bishop Javier Lozano Barragan checked to see if the photographs he had intended to take were in his briefcase. He wondered what the Pope would say when he saw them, as he looked at the photos himself one last time. Soon he would meet with John Paul II for lunch and he wanted to surprise the Holy Father.

A few months earlier, Barragan, Bishop of Zacatecas, Mexico, greeted the Holy Father at the local airport. Nearby was a married couple with a five-year-old boy. The child looked terrible. He was pale with sunken cheeks and not a single hair on his head. That is how he looked in the picture taken of him standing next to John Paul II.

Barragan had another photo with him as well, though this one had been taken very recently. The photo was of the same boy – but he was now different. His face had gained roundness and his hair had begun to return. The Mexican Archbishop wanted to show the Holy Father the older photo first, and then the second one – and that is exactly what he did when he sat down a few hours later with the Pope at lunch.

"Holy Father, do you remember this boy?" he asked, pulling out the boy's photo in which the Holy Father stood in white vestments.

The Pope looked at the picture.

"And what about it?" he asked.

Barragan then happily took out the second photograph and showed it to the Holy Father. He noticed that the Pope's facial expression changed. Up to now their conversation had flowed freely amid jokes and laughter, but seeing the second photo John Paul II's face became serious.

"God does great and miraculous things," the Pope said.

## LET GO OF THAT DOVE

*May 1990*

Maria del Refugio Mireles Badillo was certain that this was the last chance for her son. Five-year-old Heron had been in the hospital for a number of months ill with leukemia, and he was dying before her eyes. She couldn't bear to see the child's sufferings as he underwent successive rounds of chemotherapy. His spinal cord had been pierced with needles over 500 times; there was blood in his urine and he could not eat anything. He weighed only fourteen kilograms and looked more like a skeleton than a normal five-year-old.

His parents looked for help in many places. Heron had been in five hospitals before finally arriving at the National Pediatric Institute in Mexico City.

Then, they heard that the Pope was going to visit Mexico, and would even make his way to Zacatecas! This was only two hours by car from Rio Grande, where they lived. Maria felt that she had to experience being near John Paul II. Her husband did not show any great enthusiasm over it. A leftist politician, he respected the Pope but he was also an atheist. He felt that a risky trip to the airport was unlikely to do much good for Heron's condition. Maria, however, was determined to go ahead with it and saw her plan through. "If only the Holy Father would come near to us," she thought, as the Papal aircraft was about to arrive.

It was May 12, 1990. Finally, those gathered saw a dark spot in the sky that drew closer in their eyes. Soon, the plane touched down at the airport. They saw the figure of the man dressed in white. They were disappointed, however, when they noticed that the way by which the Pope was to pass was nowhere near where they happened to be standing. Their only hope was that, as often happened, John Paul II would stray from the designated route and approach people on his own accord. And so it happened: the Pope came their way! They could not believe their eyes. Heron, who was being held by his mother, was holding on tightly to a dove which he was to release on the Holy Father's command. He felt that something important was happening. Finally he saw the Holy Father up close: his gentle, smiling face, the white skullcap on his head and the cross he wore which shone brightly in the sun. What could the man want from him? The Pope raised his hand. Heron continued to hold onto the dove. The Pope repeated the gesture. The boy finally understood. The dove flapped its wings and flew off into the air.

John Paul II smiled widely. He bent over and kissed the boy's bald head. A moment later, he backed away.

"Mom, I'm hungry," said Heron once they were back inside their car.

"You're hungry? Are you sure?" asked his mother with some amazement. Over the past two weeks, Heron had been unable to eat any solid food at all and it seemed unlikely to Maria that he should now suddenly regain his appetite.

"Yes, I want some chicken," said the boy.

Could it be that Maria's feelings had not betrayed her? The more time passed from the meeting with the Holy Father at the airport in Zacatecas, the more Heron's parents felt that something extraordinary had taken place. Heron told them

Heron held a dove in his hand which he was to let go
on the Holy Father's command.

at one point that when the Pope touched him, he felt like an electrical charge had passed through him and that he suddenly gained strength. A few months later, it turned out that not a single trace of leukemia remained in Heron's body. He no longer took any medication, his hair grew back and he began to live a normal life.

## HERON TODAY

Today, Heron Badillo is an active, athletic twenty-year-old. He is 180 centimetres tall with thick hair, a short beard and an engaging disposition. One would never guess seeing him now that fifteen years earlier he was fighting for his life and suffering terribly with no guarantee that he would ever be healthy. The doctors at the Pediatric Institute in Mexico City say that his condition at the time of his release from the hospital was treatable, but they are astonished that the boy was cured of the illness since his therapy had been stopped and was never again resumed. Heron's parents believe that it was a twofold miracle: first, because the Holy Father approached them, and second, because Heron was made well.

Cardinal Javier Lozano Barragan, since 1997 the head of the Pontifical Council for the Pastoral Assistance to Health Care Workers, observes that yet another remarkable thing happened: "Heron's father used to be an atheist; he didn't even want to go with his son to the airport that day. Now, his faith is greater than mine."

On January 28, 2004, the Mexican Cardinal went with the Badillo family to Rome to thank the Holy Father in person for that meeting in Mexico. The picture from that meeting shows the same people who came out to greet the Holy Father at the airport in Zacatecas. Their roles, however, had changed somewhat: the Holy Father, himself once so strong and athletic, was now weak and ill. Heron, who in 1990 was pale, thin and bald, was now a handsome, healthy young man. "When we showed the Holy Father the picture, he immediately recalled that moment at the airport," said Heron.

"When we showed the Holy Father the picture, he immediately recalled that moment at the airport." - Nineteen-year-old Heron Badillo with his parents in audience with John Paul II, January 8, 2004.

Heron even thought about joining the priesthood. He entered a seminary but after a while realized that it wasn't his calling.

"I want to become an engineer and get married," he said, "to serve God's people in another way."

He has a girlfriend, is studying and is preparing for his exams at the university.

At the Badillo home, a photograph of the Holy Father stands prominently displayed. For them, this man was truly God's representative and a saint. Can that day in 1990 be called a miracle? Diocesan representatives in Zacatecas argue in the affirmative.

"We believe that the Pope healed that boy, who today is a healthy student," said Fr. Humberto Salinas, spokesman for the Zacatecas diocese, adding, "I am personally convinced that a miracle occurred there."

Heron said: "I put myself at the disposition of the Vatican and will gladly testify as to my healing, should such a need arise. Even if it doesn't assist the cause of his beatification, at least it should help others to not lose faith in the holiness of John Paul II."

*The truth about creation is the first and fundamental truth of our faith. It is not, however, the only one nor the supreme one. Faith teaches us that the work of creation is contained within the ambit of God's plan which, according to his intention, goes well beyond the limits of creation itself. Creation-particularly the human creature called into existence in the visible world-is open to an eternal destiny, which is fully revealed in Jesus Christ. Even in Christ the work of creation is completed by the work of salvation. Salvation means a new creation (cf. 2 Cor 5:17; Gal 6:15), a creation according to the measure of the Creator's original design.*

John Paul II
"Miracles Manifest the Supernatural Order"
General Audience, January 13, 1988

# ON THE OTHER SIDE OF THE HILL

*The year 1988*

Maria Angelica Bedoya had a difficult choice to make. For two years, from the moment of her daughter's birth, she struggled to improve the health of the child. The little girl had been born with hydrocephalus and her life was in constant danger. Doctors proposed an operation, ideally in Brazil, because the conditions did not exist in their native land of Uruguay to conduct such a complex procedure. She was to travel there in May, but at that time Pope John Paul II was to visit Paraguay. Included in the Pope's three-day itinerary was a visit to the shrine at Caacupé, where Bishop Demetrio Aquino, the young girl's godfather, lived and worked.

"Will you come?" he asked Maria Angelica. "I can help arrange a meeting with the Holy Father for you."

Maria didn't know what to do. On the one hand, she had the chance of taking her daughter to get the operation done, and on the other, she could take her to meet the Pope. Finally, she decided on the latter: Brazil was closer than Rome, and she doubted that the Pope would visit Paraguay again.

## CAACUPÉ

The name of the national shrine of Paraguay comes from the native Guarani word "caaguycupé," which means "the other side of the hill." Since the seventeenth century, worshippers have come to pray at the foot of the statue of Nuestra Señora de Los Milagres (Our Lady of Miracles), carved from wood by an Indian who had earlier converted to Christianity.

This man, who lived in the Franciscan mission in Tobati, was run down by warriors of the Mbayáes tribe, which did not convert to Christianity and treated all Christian converts as mortal enemies. Escaping from the warriors, the fugitive saw a large tree. He hid in its stump and, terrorized, begged the Virgin Mary to spare his life. He promised that were he to survive he would carve a statue of the Blessed Virgin from the wood of this same tree that sheltered him from the deadly attack. He was able to keep his promise, as the warriors pursuing him were not able to find him.

Subsequently, the spared man carved two figures: the larger of the two ended up at the mission in Tobati while he kept the smaller one for himself.

In 1603, an enormous flood hit the Pirayú valley. The natural disaster swept away the fixture that held the statue of the Blessed Virgin. But when the waters receded, it was discovered that the statue itself had not been destroyed; in fact it had not even moved from its place. From that time on, the cult of Our Lady of Miracles began. A local carpenter erected a small chapel and pilgrims began arriving shortly thereafter.

Almost 400 years later, Pope John Paul II concluded his pilgrimage to Paraguay in that very location.

It was a nice birthday present for the Holy Father. He was turning 68 and was about to visit one of the most significant Marian shrines in all of South America. The Pope lent much importance to places of Marian devotion all over the world. Already for some time he had been travelling spiritually across the globe and mentioning Marian shrines during the Sunday Angelus. Now the Holy Father had the chance to actually be in Caacupé to conclude this difficult trip to Paraguay.

Why the difficulties? For many years, Paraguay was ruled by Alfred Stroessner, a ruthless dictator. The Pope knew from local bishops about the many abuses of power. And many times the Bishop of Rome had demanded justice.

A sad incident occurred during the Papal visit itself. On the second day of his stay, the Holy Father was to meet with the so-called "builders of society". These were people involved in the creation of culture, upbringing of the youth, developing agriculture and politics. At the last moment, the Paraguayan interior minister called off the meeting. Holy See Press Office Director Joaquin Navarro-Valls criticized this as a decision without precedent in the history of the Pope's pastoral service and expressed his absolute amazement in the face of it. Finally, the Paraguayan government relented and the Pope was able to meet with the "builders of society".

The following day, May 18, 1988, the Holy Father entrusted all of Paraguay's hardships over to its Patroness in Caacupé. He especially wanted to address the farmers and give them his attention. The local Bishop had intervened on their behalf occasionally before. And following the murder of Arturo Bernala, head of a cooperative and father of four, Bishop Demetrio Aquino, wrote a much publicized letter to the government: "I am certain that Our Lady of Caacupé and our Lord Jesus Christ will ensure that those responsible for this dreadful act of cruelty will regret bitterly what they have done, and that the revered Mother of all Paraguayans will see to it that the guilty ones are punished appropriately."

Most of all, though, the Holy Father wanted to do the same thing here as he had done so often before at other shrines around the world: entrust the nation to Mary. He deeply believed in the effectiveness of such acts. Many times, he was convinced that situations that look hopeless from a human point of view were resolved when one gave everything over in trust to Divine Providence.

## MARIA ANGELICA

Bedoya shook nervously as she held her daughter in her hands. The child bore the same names as her mother, but in reverse order. Two-year-old Angelica Maria was restless; she moved about and cried, attracting the displeasure of those standing around waiting for the Pope in the sacristy of the church in Caacupé. Four o'clock in the afternoon was approaching. Maria Angelica heard applause and figured that the Pope must be nearby. A few moments later, he indeed appeared in the sacristy. Next to him was Bishop Aquino.

"Holy Father, this is the little girl that I spoke to Your Holiness about," he said, pointing to Angelica Maria.

The Pope approached closer. He stretched out his hand and put it on the little girl's head. The child calmed down. The Holy Father prayed for a moment and then walked away to prepare for Mass.

The meeting between the Holy Father and the little girl lasted no more than a few minutes. Not long after, the ceremony began. Maria Angelica, happy that her daughter was so calm now, listened to the homily in which the Pope spoke about the Marian geography of Paraguay. The Holy Father could not avoid pointing out the fact that Paraguay was the only country whose cities bear the names of events in the life of the Blessed Virgin Mary: Concepción (Conception), Encarnación (Incarnation), Asunción (Assumption).

"Caacupé constitutes the centre of this Marian geography," said John Paul II, "so beautifully expressed in the names of your cities, forever reminding us of three main Marian mysteries." The Pope also said that this place had been chosen by the Mother of God, "to which the history of this shrine has provided signs and testimonies." Maria Angelica didn't yet know that she was coddling in her arms living proof of the truth of what the Holy Father was saying.

A month later, the little girl was set to undergo an operation. To the amazement of the doctors, this was the last medical intervention in the course of her illness: the hydrocephalus had disappeared completely. Angelica Maria grew into a healthy, attractive and athletic young woman. Each year she gets tested medically and each year the diagnosis is the same, with the doctors telling her that she is perfectly healthy.

She is not only healthy but is a gifted student. In 2004 she completed high school with honours, entered her first-year studies in law and is a dance instructor on top of that.

She never saw the Pope up close again and does not remember the meeting in the sacristy at the Caacupé shrine.

Her mother told her many times about the prayer of John Paul II and how she immediately calmed down and felt better afterwards.

"I regret that the Holy Father never came back to Paraguay after that," said Angelica Maria, "and that I wasn't able to travel to Rome. But despite that, he remains very close to me."

*After the resurrection, ascension and pentecost, the "miracles-signs" performed by Christ were continued by the apostles, and later by the saints from generation to generation. The Acts of the Apostles offer us numerous testimonies concerning miracles worked "in the name of Jesus Christ" by Peter (cf. Acts 3:1-8; 5:15; 9:32-41), Stephen (Acts 6:8) and Paul (e.g., Acts 14:8-10). We also see it in the lives of the saints, the history of the Church and in particular, the processes for the canonization of the Servants of God. These constitute a documentation which, when submitted to the most searching examination of historical criticism and of medical science, confirms the existence of the "power from on high" which operates in the natural order and surpasses it.*

John Paul II
"Miracles Manifest the Supernatural Order"
General Audience, January 13, 1988

# CELEBRATING
# HER VOWS

*Venezuela, 1984*

"I have a wonderful present for you, Sister, on the golden anniversary of your vows to religious life." Mother Superior glanced smiling at the older nun who had come to her office a moment earlier. "Fifty years in the convent – now that's a wonderful milestone. You work with such dedication, Sister; you never travel and you never see the world outside our own convent. I therefore thought that as a present we would send you on a trip to Europe. We can go together since I've never been there yet either."

Ofelia Trespalacios sighed quietly.

"But Mother," she answered, "I am so ill. The present is fantastic but it's not for me. I regret that I can't accept. This illness is killing me."

Sister Ofelia had just turned seventy. For five years she had suffered from nausea and dizziness. The doctors thought the cause to be an inner-ear disturbance, but neither a stay at the hospital in Caracas nor Támesis did anything to improve her condition. "It's incurable," the doctors would say, eventually throwing up their hands in despair.

"In Spain there are excellent specialists," said Mother Superior. "Maybe they will be able to track down the source of your problem, Sister, and then you can get the right medicine. A change in environment might also be helpful for you. I am convinced that you should come along."

"As a matter of obedience?" asked the nun, for although it was over 50 years since she made her vows entering the community of the Sisters of Poverty of St. Peter Clavier, she remembered them well and held fast to them: chastity, poverty and obedience – the three evangelical counsels of Jesus, which when practiced faithfully were to lead to holiness in consecrated life.

"Yes," said Mother Superior. "It will do you a lot of good."

After many years, Ofelia was to leave the house in Gautire where the Sisters ran a refuge for poor Indian children and the elderly. A few months later – it was 1985 – she was in Madrid. From there she took a night train to Rome. The Eternal City appealed greatly to Ofelia, but the joys of discovering Christianity's capital city were overshadowed by her recurring health problems. Finally the day came when the Sisters were to meet with the Pope. Around ten o'clock in the morning, the group of Sisters gathered outside the Pope's residence at Castel Gandolfo. They were not alone; many Bishops and Cardinals were standing in the hallway since there wasn't room for everyone in the Papal chapel. The entire liturgy was therefore planned for outside.

Ofelia stood together with fifteen other Sisters who had come from all over Europe and waited with them to see the Pope.

Finally, the Holy Father appeared. Ofelia saw him well, though she found herself in the rear of the group. She was able to come closer and even receive Communion from the Pope's hands. Afterwards, she and the rest of the Sisters stepped off to the left side to wait for their meeting with John Paul II. Less than twenty minutes later, the Pope approached them and began to hand out rosaries.

Sister Trespalacios was standing in the second row. She was considerably taller than the other Sisters and she didn't want to block their view. She observed John Paul II as he slowly moved towards her. Their eyes met for a moment. The Holy Father extended his hand in which he held a rosary. She held out her hand and tightly grasped the Pope's hand.

"Holy Father, bless me," she said. "My illness isn't letting me live. Please pray that it might go away."

The Pope smiled, took her hand and whispered to her: "Pray."

How was she to pray to God in this moment? The idea came to her that she should say a prayer of repentance. The Pope let go of her hand, lightly patted her cheek, blessed her and prayed silently for a few moments. He then let down his hands, smiled and gave her a rosary.

"I felt as if my hair were standing on end and there was a warmth expanding all over my body," recalled Sister Trespalacios. "From that moment, my dizzy spells disappeared forever. I immediately thought: 'That was Jesus who put His hands on me. He's a saint! The very hand of Jesus healed me.'"


Ofelia Trespalacios visited Rome in 1985 and returned home without any trace of illness.

"I used to visit the hospital so often, but the best doctor I ever had was the Holy Father," she recalled twenty years later.

When John Paul II died, Ofelia was ninety years old. She is convinced that John Paul II is a saint.

*alvation means a new creation (cf. 2 Cor 5:17; Gal 6:15), a creation according to the measure of the Creator's original design. Salvation means a re-establishment of what God had made and which in human history had suffered the disorder and "corruption" following upon sin.*

*Christ's miracles enter into the project of the "new creation" and are therefore linked to the order of salvation. They are the salvific signs which call to conversion and to faith, and in this way, to the renewal of the world that is subject to "corruption" (cf. Rom 8:19-21).*

John Paul II
"Miracles Manifest the Supernatural Order"
General Audience, January 13, 1988

John Paul II at the Divine Mercy Shrine, Cracow,
Łagiewniki, Poland, August 17, 2002.

# PRAY TO MY SISTER FAUSTINA

He had had enough. Was it even possible that one could live without pain, to be able to walk freely and enjoy life? The longer he lived, the less likely this seemed to him. He was sick, is sick and will be sick for the rest of his days. Multiple sclerosis, muscular dystrophy and epilepsy – wasn't all this too much for a young man under forty years of age? Adding to the misery, there were serious difficulties with his eyesight and spinal cord.

Ugo Festa experienced the world exclusively from a wheelchair.

He was born in Vicenza, Italy, in 1951. Pain, suffering and a lack of hope that he would ever be well had been with him from early childhood. He had seen many specialists but none of them could propose a way to treat his illnesses. They readily told him that in his situation only prayer for a miracle could help him. Ugo, however, didn't believe in such things. All the same, he decided to travel to Lourdes just to prove to those who advised him to pray that it was nothing but a big superstition. Once there, though, he experienced something surprising. He was not healed, but gained the conviction that God does indeed exist.

Some years later Ugo heard that a pilgrimage was to travel from his town to Rome for the beatification of Fr. Filipo Rinaldi, a Salesian. Ugo joined the pilgrimage.

The group arrived in the Eternal City on April 28, 1990. Ugo Festa was overjoyed because he was introduced to Mother Teresa of Calcutta. The founder of the Missionaries of Charity bent down over him, gave him a hug and said some words of encouragement to him. Ugo sat in his wheelchair.

"Maybe you'd like to come to the retreat in Trent with us?" asked one of the Sisters once Mother Teresa walked away. The Sister was a member of the same group present at the gathering.

Ugo shook his head, indicating that he wasn't interested. Why would he want to go there?

"There is a shrine dedicated to the Divine Mercy there," the Sister explained, inviting him once more to go with them.

"No, I'll stay in Rome," answered Ugo.

"At least take this," said the Sister, taking a medallion and some pictures out of her bag. Ugo looked at the image of Jesus, whose left hand was pointing to the area of His heart from which two rays of light emanated: one white and one red. At the bottom were the words, Gesù, confido in Te (Jesus, I trust in You).

"That's an image of the Divine Mercy," explained the Sister, as she and Ugo parted ways.

The next day, Ugo was at St. Peter's Square with other sick people waiting for the Pope, who traditionally stopped by those sitting in wheelchairs. Seeing John Paul II, Ugo extended to him the images and medallion that he had received.

"Holy Father, please bless them," he said.

The Holy Father made the sign of the cross over the items and bent down over Ugo.

"How do you feel?" the Holy Father asked him.

"Terrible. I am living through a terrible crisis."

The Pope looked into Ugo's desperate face. He then looked at the images that Ugo held.

"How can you say that while holding an image of the Divine Mercy in your hand?" the Pope asked him, smiling lightly. "Entrust yourself to Him and pray to my Sister Faustina asking for her intercession."

Watching the figure of the Pope dressed in white as he walked away, Ugo recalled the invitation to the retreat in Trent from the day before. "Maybe I should go," he thought. He went that same year.

For the next three days, Ugo appeared before the painting of the Divine Mercy at the side altar in the church of Villa O'Santissima Villazzano in Trent. He returned there on the fourth day. He sat in his wheelchair and gazed at the life-sized figure of Jesus on the canvas.

There was a twitch in his body. No! That's impossible … yet he saw that Jesus was putting His hands out to him. Ugo felt a wave of warmth passing through him and suddenly the awareness came over him that he was standing upright before the painting of the Lord and had his arms stretched out toward it. At that moment he saw that the figure dressed in a white robe was coming down towards him. "My God, that's the Man from Galilee, He's coming to me!" Ugo thought. He then heard the words, "Get up and walk!" And he began to walk. He understood at that moment that he was completely well. Still not completely sure that it was real, he ran out of the church. It was not a hallucination: there was not a single trace of his illness left!

This happened to someone who for many years dismissed the very idea of God. He understood that he didn't want to listen to Him even as he was on a pilgrimage to Rome. After all, Ugo might not have come to Trent at all. He recalled the invitation of the Sister after he met Mother Teresa. At the time, the invitation of some nun seemed rather insignificant, but now he looked at it completely differently. He was convinced that it was God Himself who had invited him, to which he had initially said "no". It had to take the words of the Pope for Ugo to change his mind.

Ugo knew that he had to tell John Paul II about what had happened. On August 19, 1990, during the General Audience, Ugo was able to get close to the Holy Father and tell him about his healing.

He then left Rome, first travelling to India where he volunteered as a nurse for Mother Teresa and the Missionaries of

Image of the Divine Mercy at St. Peter's Square.
Canonization of Sr. Faustina, April 30, 2000.

Charity. Later he went to Africa to work among the poor there. Finally, he arrived back in Vicenza, the place of so many of his sufferings. Ugo's hometown had been witness to his illness and pain. Now, Ugo organized a hospice for the neediest and those living on the margins of society.

That is what he was doing in 2005.


Then, Ugo learned that he had cancer. Still, he was not devastated, saying, "What should I worry about? Jesus saved me once, so everything will be fine again."

He wasn't healed, but it was not the cancer that took his life. On May 22, 2005, he was found in a pool of blood, his head torn apart by bullets from a revolver. A week later, two individuals were arrested on charges of murder.

Ugo Festa lived only a month and a half longer than the man who fifteen years earlier told him to entrust himself to the Divine Mercy. John Paul II died April 2, 2005, on the Saturday following the first Sunday of Easter. On the Pope's decision, Divine Mercy Sunday is celebrated on the Second Sunday of Easter. "His Sister," St. Faustina, noted a full fourteen times in her diary that that was in fact the day chosen by Jesus for the Feast of Divine Mercy.

*It is a question of miraculous signs carried out from apostolic times until the present day. Their essential purpose is to indicate that the human person is destined and called to the kingdom of God. These signs therefore confirm in different ages and in the most varied circumstances the truth of the Gospel, and demonstrate the saving power of Christ who does not cease to call people (through the Church) on the path of faith.*

John Paul II
"Miracles Manifest the Supernatural Order"
General Audience, January 13, 1988

# YOUR SHRINE
# IS ESPECIALLY
# CLOSE AND DEAR
# TO ME

Father Mirosław Drozdek, a Pallotine, didn't know whether to laugh or to cry. He had just received word that the Papal Nuncio to Poland, Archbishop Józef Kowalczcyk, had announced plans for Pope John Paul II's sixth pilgrimage to Poland. In the program for the visit was something that would satisfy the dreams of all the residents of Zakopane and of Fr. Drozdek himself. For many years, the priest had overseen the building of Our Lady of Fatima Church in Krzeptówki, a shrine erected as a gesture of thanksgiving for the election of Karol Wojtyła to the throne of St. Peter and his miraculous survival of the assassination attempt of May 13, 1981. Now, John Paul II would come himself to consecrate this shrine in Poland's Highland region! The Holy Father would stay for a full three days in the main Highland city. The consecration of the church in Krzeptówki was planned for the final day of the Papal visit, Saturday, June 7.

However, Fr. Drozdek was worried. For almost twenty years, he had been suffering from a worsening throat problem. It was getting progressively harder for him to speak, not to mention sing. Could a priest with vocal difficulties prepare such an important ceremony? It seemed impossible. Fr. Drozdek decided that should he not get better he would resign from his position as custodian of the shrine.

All attempts to treat Fr. Drozdek's condition ended in failure. Once, he even travelled to Switzerland to try a special curative procedure at the place where two weeks earlier Margaret Thatcher, ex-Prime Minister of Great Britain, had received treatment. But Fr. Drozdek's condition did not improve. As if that wasn't enough, doctors found a growth in his vocal chords. They called for immediate surgery. A date was set for the procedure, which was to take place at the laryngological clinic in Katowice.

Shortly before the operation, Fr. Drozdek picked up the phone and called Fr. Stanisław Dziwisz.

"I'm sick and am going to have an operation," he said. "If the Holy Father can't help me, then nobody can."

"Come," Fr. Drozdek heard.

Less than twenty hours later, he was in Rome. The next day he was in the famous Papal chapel at the Vatican. The first time he prayed here was February 14, 1979 – four months after the election of Karol Wojtyła to the throne of St. Peter. From that time, Fr. Drozdek had been a frequent guest, especially after May 13, 1981. It was on that day that, at 9:30 p.m., the Highlanders decided to dedicate the church in Krzeptówki as a gesture of thanksgiving that the Pope's life might be saved. Thereafter, Fr. Drozdek travelled to the Vatican to give progress reports and to show floor plans and photos of the ongoing construction of the church.

The priest observed how John Paul II immersed himself completely in prayer prior to Mass. He had the impression of the Pope not really being there at all. "Father of prayer," he thought to himself, recalling the biblical account of Moses talking to God on Mount Sinai.

Mass, then thanksgiving; the Holy Father prayed for a long time still. Finally he got up off his knees and walked over to the nearby room where Fr. Dziwisz had earlier brought the custodian of the shrine in Zakopane.

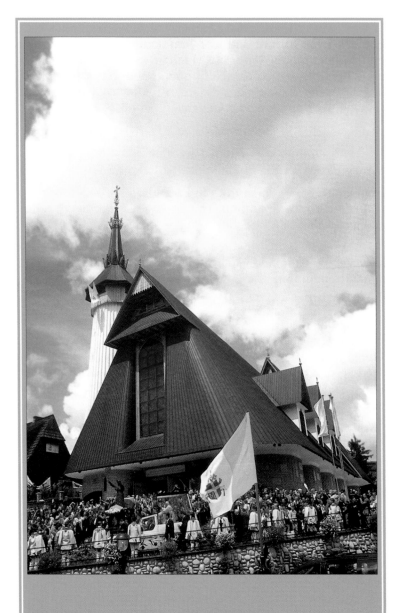

Our Lady of Fatima church
in Krzeptówki, Zakopane, Poland.

"I was alone with the Holy Father," recalled Fr. Drozdek. "I knelt in front of him and told him about the situation. The Holy Father touched my neck. I felt an immense sense of energy and heat, which passed through my throat. I felt dazed. The Pope left. Some minutes later, Fr. Dziwisz came back. I was still somewhat dizzy when standing up."

"That's normal – you have to wait," Dziwisz said.

"Fifteen minutes later I left. I felt that something was happening to me. I still couldn't speak although I felt better."

Immediately upon his return to Poland, Fr. Drozdek went to Katowice for the operation. The growth was removed. A day and a half later, Fr. Drozdek asked to be released.

"You must be mad," the head of the ward told the priest. "I have yet to see someone leave the hospital so soon after such a major operation," she said.

"Please believe me ... I really feel much better," the patient answered. "I need to be on a radio show soon and I've got to get back to my place."

Things had improved to the point that Fr. Drozdek was indeed able to thank listeners for their prayers in his intention. He was convinced then and remains convinced today that it was the Holy Father who did the most on his behalf.

"At the very time that I lay on the operating table, the Holy Father celebrated Mass in my intention. I am positive that the procedure itself was just the final touch in my healing, which began with his prayers."

Fr. Drozdek had believed in the power of John Paul II's prayers for a long time already. Three years earlier, Fr. Drozdek had encountered severe difficulties with the construction of the shrine.

"In human terms, it was basically impossible," he recalled. "I can't go into details because the people who were causing the difficulties are still alive. I called Fr. Dziwisz at the time and told him everything. Soon afterwards I had the opportunity to be at the Vatican. I wanted to ask the Holy Father for his prayers. However, after Mass he turned to me on his own and said: 'Don't worry, Father. All will be well.'"

A couple of weeks later, the problems ceased.

"That taught me that one has to believe and ask humbly," said Fr. Drozdek.

It was for that reason that he went to the Pope first upon hearing that he would have to undergo an operation. He believes that it was thanks to the Holy Father's intervention that the disease went away and never returned – even though the diagnosis had been a malignant growth. In June of 1997, Fr. Drozdek greeted the Pope in the very spot where the Highlanders had prayed for the Holy Father's life to be saved and where they had invited him many times.

"Your shrine in Krzeptówki is especially close and dear to me," said John Paul II. "You worship Our Lady of Fatima here. What took place at St. Peter's Square on May 13, 1981, is connected to the history of this shrine. On that day I experienced an imminent threat to my life and suffering, but I also experienced God's great Mercy. My life was spared thanks to Our Lady of Fatima. After my stay at Gemelli hospital, I became aware of the prayers and wishes of people all over the world in my intention – especially the prayers. My thoughts turned to the first Christians, who prayed in earnest to God for St. Peter when his life was in danger (see Acts 12:5).

"I know how deeply Zakopane participated in the worldwide prayer of the Church. I know that you gathered in your local parishes as well as in Our Lady of Fatima chapel in Krzeptówki to pray the rosary, asking for health and strength for the Pope. Then, too, was born the idea to build the church at this site, at the foot of Giewont – a shrine to Our Lady of Fatima as a gesture of thanksgiving for saving my life. I know that this shrine, which I consecrate here today, was erected by many hands and hearts working together in sacrifice and love for the Pope. It's hard to talk about without being moved..."

"Your shrine in Krzeptówki is especially close and dear to me."
- John Paul II at Our Lady of Fatima church
in Krzeptówki, Zakopane, Poland. June 7, 1997.

In March 2005, as John Paul II lay in Gemelli hospital, Highlanders led by Fr. Drozdek rallied again in prayer, asking God to save the Pope.

"In February Sister Lucia died. She was the last of the Fatima visionaries," recalled Fr. Drozdek. "We quietly hoped that her prayers would bring about a miracle from heaven that would in effect also help her cause for sainthood. But things happened differently. I later recalled a certain situation from her funeral, in which I participated. The last moments of Sister Lucia's life and her very last words were actually recorded on video. She said at that time: 'We're going, we're going to heaven ... with the Holy Father, the shepherds, the angels and with the Heart of Jesus.' Those words were written down on a picture that was prepared for her funeral. At first it didn't seem right to me: here we were praying for the Holy Father's recovery, while at Sister Lucia's funeral there was a picture with such a caption. We talked about it after the funeral with the organizers. They had already decided to leave out those words, but later decided that it wouldn't be right to do so. It was a lesson in humility. People have their thoughts and desires, but we mustn't interfere with that which comes from on high. Later, it became even more clear: the Pope's words, 'Let me go to the Father's house' and his death on the first Saturday of the month when the devotion to the Immaculate Heart of Mary is observed (as per the Fatima proclamation) left no doubt in my mind that this was exactly what was meant to happen.

*This saving power of the God-Man is manifested also when the "miracles-signs" are performed through the intercession of individuals, of saints, of devout people – just as the first sign at Cana of Galilee was worked through the intercession of the Mother of Christ.*

John Paul II
"Miracles Manifest the Supernatural Order"
General Audience, January 13, 1988

"…here at the Grotto of Massabielle, I am moved by the feeling
that I have arrived at the destination of my pilgrimage."
- John Paul II in Lourdes, August 14, 2004.]

# DOCTOR
# OF MIRACLES

**Lourdes**, a shrine in the French Pyrenees, is famous for many healings and conversions. It was also the place of John Paul II's very last international trip: the Holy Father stayed there August 14-15, 2004.

"Kneeling here at the Grotto of Massabielle, I am moved by the feeling that I have reached the destination of my pilgrimage!" said John Paul II upon arriving at the shrine. He then lit a candle and took a drink of the water from the spring that was formed there 146 years earlier.

On February 11, 1858, the Virgin Mary appeared for the first time to fourteen-year-old Bernadette Soubirous. Additional visions followed. On February 25, the Lady in White showed the young girl where she was to dig that the spring may gush forth. "Go drink from this spring and wash yourselves in it," heard Bernadette. Four years later, the visions were officially approved by the Church. Lourdes became a focal point of pilgrimages, especially for the sick, while February 11 was proclaimed World Day of the Sick by the Polish Pope.

"Lourdes, called the 'shrine of human suffering' by John Paul II, welcomed His Holiness, himself among the ill and suffering, on Saturday," Radio France Internationale reported on August 14, 2004. Among the eyewitnesses of the Pope's visit to Lourdes was Dr. Patrick Theillier. Dr. Theillier is the twelfth director of the Medical Bureau of Our Lady of Lourdes – the place where people go who report that they have been healed of various ailments. As such, he has been called the "Doctor of Miracles".

A year after the visit of John Paul II to Lourdes and half a year after his death, I spoke to Dr. Theillier about miracles, the Pope and his relationship to the Lourdes Shrine.

"For him this was a very important place. The best proof of this is the fact that he wanted to come here before he died," said Dr. Theillier. "I remember the moment when the Holy Father got off the Popemobile and knelt on the kneeler – he very nearly fell over. Some thought that it was due to his weakness or his illness … yet in fact he was greatly moved emotionally."

**"John Paul II then met with the many sick who were there…"**

"I can say that immediately after the Holy Father left, a woman who had been healed came to the Medical Bureau. She was originally from Marseilles, was married and had two children. Twenty years earlier she succumbed to a serious car accident. She suffered a spinal injury, had to wear a corset and would experience terrible migraines every couple of days. Before going to sleep she had to take painkillers and lay her pillow down a certain way each time so as to minimize the pain. Then, in August, she came to Lourdes. At the very moment she heard Pope John Paul II say 'I bless you,' she felt her illness disappear. That same evening, after twenty years, she fell asleep without any painkillers and without setting her pillow as before. On August 17, two days after the Holy Father's departure from Lourdes, she came to us and announced that she had been made well. I remain in contact with her. A year has passed since that event and she continues to be well. A lot has changed in her life. She works with the sick in hospitals, and helps the sick who pilgrimage to Lourdes."

**"What needs to happen for a miracle to take place?"**

"In every instance, the initiative comes from God. It doesn't depend on the holiness of the person experiencing the cure. The person to whom it happens is dumbfounded. The person doesn't even have to be a Catholic – many atheists and Muslims have experienced cures at Lourdes. What does count is the faith of God's people who gather in this extraordinary place. Prayer also counts, as does the love of those helping others."

**"You mentioned the faithful gathered in the Shrine. John Paul II frequently visited shrines but also appeared in places that weren't connected to a religious tradition. There, he gathered around himself great numbers of people. Is that also a likely setting for the occurrence of a miracle?"**

"Healings can take place wherever 'two or three are gathered in Jesus' name.'"

**"How would you define a miracle?"**

"It's an event connected to God, who wishes good upon people. We generally view miracles as the impossible actually taking place. Most importantly, though, miracles are signs from God, who is active around us. The physical healing is a tangible fact but it forms only part of what we call a miracle. The second part is the meaning given to the occurrence. In the *Petit Robert* dictionary miracles are described as supernatural events that show the benevolence of God and to which spiritual meaning is ascribed."

**"What, then, is the spiritual significance of a miracle?"**

"It depends first of all on how we understand the workings of God in the universe. As we know, there are atheists who question God's existence and agnostics who don't really think about it at all. One can believe in God and be convinced that He exists wholly outside of our world. In our cultural milieu, God is often treated like an original mover who set the world into motion and then cut himself off from it. Christianity, however, believes otherwise: humanity is loved by God, who will do everything to show His love for us, especially through signs. Miracles are one example of such signs.

We often don't notice these signs because in our materially developed society we tend to believe that what matters is what we ourselves have or can do: Are we strong? Do we have money in the bank? Do we have adequate material means? Because of this, we have lost the sense of the sacred – something that remains to a large degree, for example, in Africa. When I meet with Africans at various conferences, they tell me that there are many miracles in their native lands. "We don't even mention them much," they say, "because so many of them occur. We don't have the medicines that are available in the West, so we pray over the sick and they get healed."

### "How can we know what is a miracle and what isn't?"

"Of course, it's very difficult to test the testimony of someone who was sick and then believes that he's been made well. I've met many such people. A great deal of judgment is required. You see a person externally, but these happenings concern their internal lives. Even healings – physical miracles – are external signs of things that happened internally. One feels a very strong working of God inside oneself; it is as though God passes through one. I personally believe that miraculous healings are personal encounters with Jesus, the One who heals. Such encounters can be very simple and don't need to include extraordinary signs. Occasionally, however, external signs do occur – and that's when the power of God is plainly visible.

It's also noteworthy that there are ordinary and extraordinary miracles. For example, it's a miracle that God sustains the world; that the sun rises at a given time; that we are alive. We don't notice these miracles as such because we have become accustomed to them. There are also extraordinary miracles that 'make more noise,' if I can put it that way. In either case, they are signs from God.

**"Why does God use them?"**

"Because He wants us to be free and to be able to choose; He gives signs but does not force us to do anything. Miracles don't force anyone to believe, but they can help those who are open to faith. Divine signs point to our freedom: we can take them into account or we can deny them. It's all up to us.

**"Isn't believing in miracles like believing in magic?"**

"Those are two different things. Those who dabble in magic want to be masters by tapping into supernatural powers to achieve their own goals. A miracle in Christianity is something else entirely: we receive it without doing anything to deserve it. In magic, pride rules one's actions. When it comes to miracles, humble acceptance is key.

**"Do miracles, or signs having to do with John Paul II, make a case for his holiness?"**

"One of the characteristics of saints who are still alive on earth is that they are changed in nature. This is well seen in the story of St. Francis who tamed the wolf that was terrorizing the people of Gubbio. We, too, feel touched and transformed when in the presence of someone who is filled with God's grace. It can be said that the very surroundings, even nature itself, is affected in the vicinity of a holy person. This is one of the reasons for the call to holiness: through the holiness of each person, the world itself is transformed. Holiness goes beyond the bounds of the material realm and its laws; this is seen clearly through extraordinary events."

**"It so happens that there are people who believe in the power of the Holy Father's prayers and accord them key meaning but they also make use of medical assistance. Someone had a tumour, met with the Pope, asked for his prayers; later he underwent an operation and was made well. It's a miracle, isn't it?"**

"Medicine and miracles are not opposed to each other. God works through many channels – it could be through a holy person or through ordinary human means. There really is no dichotomy.

**"In your opinion, why was the specific intervention of John Paul II effective?"**

"Saints have gifts called charisms – in Greek charisma means grace; a gift of the Holy Spirit for building up the community of the faithful. There are people who have been given the gift of healing. What they have isn't a method or technique – it's a gift. Personally, I don't think that John Paul II had the gift of healing … but he undoubtedly had the gifts of prayer, intervention and mediation.

*aking an interest in another person begins with the bishop's prayer, his talking to Christ, who entrusts His flock to him. Prayer prepares us for meeting others. These are meetings which, thanks to spiritual openness, we are able to get to know one and understand one another, even when there is little time. I pray for everyone with each passing day. When I meet someone I am already praying for him, and this helps me in my contact with that person.*

John Paul II,
*Rise, Let Us Be on Our Way*

Danuta and Stanislaw Rybicki, friends of Karol Wojtyła from the days of his academic ministry, during their last meeting with John Paul II at the Vatican. January 2005.

# Chapter 3.

# "I PRAY. THOSE ARE MYSTERIES."

Can the Pope get lost at the Vatican? Although it seems unlikely, it actually did happen on a number of occasions. Once, the Holy Father was late for an official audience that began at eleven in the morning. Most days, between eleven o'clock in the morning and one o'clock in the afternoon, John Paul II would receive important people from around the world. Yet one day he could not be located.

"We found him in the hall; he was gazing intensely at a painting of the Madonna on the wall," recalled Fr. Vincent Tran Ngoc Thu, secretary to Pope John Paul II from 1988 to 1996 (he died in 2002). "The Holy Father looked like a young child gazing at his mother. Another time, on an unusually cold December evening, a person of importance was on the line calling the Holy Father, but we couldn't find him. In desperation I walked out onto the terrace outside – that's where he was! He was kneeling in front of a small altar which bore the image of Our Lady of Fatima. Her head was covered in a dark veil."

"Your Holiness," I interrupted, "There's an urgent telephone call to the Holy Father." The Pope continued to pray in the cold and the rain.

Fr. Vincent Tran Ngoc Thu confirmed that such moments of Papal "detachment" were not at all uncommon. Describing the prayer of John Paul II, the Vietnamese priest stressed that the Pope was always first to enter the chapel before the morning Mass and would lose himself in prayer.

"He prayed with passion, his eyes closed; sometimes he let out short phrases like 'My Lord, my God!'," recalled Fr. Ngoc Thu. "The Pope treated very seriously those who wrote to him with personal prayer requests. The Papal secretaries and Sisters would sort out and arrange the requests and then present them to the Holy Father.

In John Paul II's kneeler was a compartment where the prayers of people from all across the world were left.

"Once, we received a letter from an American woman whose seventeen-year-old son had been in a coma following a diving accident," the Papal secretary recalled. "The Pope also remembers local churches in his prayers, bishops, the living and the dead. He prays intensely, pausing on each intention with his eyes closed, losing himself to contemplation."

"I remember how once we were leaving the Papal apartments and Archbishop Stanisław Dziwisz was leading us through adjacent rooms at the Aposotolic Palace," recalled Fr. Ireneusz Skubiś, chief editor of *Niedziela* magazine. "At one point he stopped and said, 'This is where the Holy Father often prays - oh, how much he prays here!'"

John Paul II's relationship with God even made impressions on people who did not share his faith. Canadian journalist Michael Valpy described himself as "a liberal, left-leaning North American," and to leave nothing to doubt, added, "and I'm not a Roman Catholic." Asked what he found most interesting about John Paul II, he answered:

"For me, it's his mysticism, his following John of the Cross, his mystical relationship with St. Stanislaus and his spiritual and national ties to Poland. It moves me a lot since I am also drawn by the mysticism of John of the Cross although I am a romantic rationalist. For the first time ever, the Pope surprised me completely in the Holy Land. I couldn't understand why he wanted to visit and revere so-called holy places that are clearly false from an historical perspective. I couldn't understand his constant prayer, those audiences with God. When I read more about his life, I began to understand more about his person, his inner being. There is much more to the story of John Paul II than what was publicized in the media during his pontificate. George Weigel was correct when he noted that the American press presented John Paul II as if he were a politician. He's not a politician – he's a mystic, a Pole who lived through Nazi and communist regimes; he's an Eastern-European intellectual."

Towards the end of John Paul II's life, his prayer surprised great numbers of people who watched those audiences with God, either on television or during pilgrimages, as did Michael Valpy. Popular belief is solid that the Pope's prayer was extremely effective. What was this prayer like, and from where did it get its strength?

# A HIDDEN MOTOR

*Yesterday I went to see "Król-Duch" (King Spirit) and now I wish to sincerely apologize as I'm being treated today. I have to be at Mass in the morning in Dębniki and later in the afternoon I have to cover my throat again so that I'll be able to speak at our Mass tomorrow.*

*Maybe God had His finger on this all along in order that I not go to tonight's anniversary gathering. I understand it as "I should be part of Your works, just as a priest should be in life in general: a hidden, unknown motor." Despite all appearances to the contrary, that is the main role of the priesthood. Hidden motors get the strongest of transmissions going. So, let that thought represent me tonight. I entrust you to God.*

*Karol*

The above was a letter received by Mieczysław Kotlarczyk from Fr. Karol Wojtyła shortly after his ordination to the priesthood in November 1946. The priest was explaining to his friend why he had been absent at the reception for the Rhapsody Theatre, which was celebrating its fifth anniversary in early November of that year. At the same time, though, he mentioned his presence at a special Mass for the theatre community in Wawel. This was probably the first written testimony of the future Pope with respect to how he saw his role in the priesthood: "a hidden, unknown motor." In that same letter, Fr. Wojtyła wrote about a first Mass following the ordination that took place in Dębniki in St. Stanislaus Kostka. That is where he met Jan Tyranowski, a tailor, mystic and apostle – and the first father of spirituality for Karol and for many others.

Thanks to him, the young men of St. Stanislaus Kostka began to discover the fact that there exists within the human being a fascinating interior life. Tyranowski showed them – as Karol Wojtyła himself would later note – that "God is in us not that we might squeeze Him into the tight confines of our human spirit, but rather that He might release us from within ourselves ... [Jan] wanted to form and cultivate that inner godliness within the person; he wanted to uncover it and show it to all his young companions."

He remembered that lesson very well. Over the years, those within Karol Wojtyła's sphere developed the conviction that his interior life was uncommonly intense as if he were constantly conversing with God. That's why so many asked for his prayers, which he did not refuse.

# FOLLOWING HIS PATH IN CRACOW

She was certain that the time had come. She had things ready a long time ago, so now she just packed everything into the small suitcase that she took with her on short trips. She then called her husband.

"Leszek, it's started," she said. "I'm going to the hospital on Kopernik Street."

She put on her coat, took her suitcase and closed the door behind her. Thankfully, the taxi stop was not far away. With some difficulty she sat down on the back seat and gave the driver the address to the hospital.

The driver glanced at her and, noticing her condition, thought that she might give birth on the spot.

"Don't worry," she said. "I feel just fine. The most important thing is that we get there safely."

Aleksandra Ludwikowska really did feel fine. Even her friends and family were surprised. They thought that having her fourth child would mean that she'd be exhausted, yet she was full of energy. She hadn't even had to visit the doctor too often. She just wanted to make sure that a well-known mid-wife in Cracow by the name of Ms. Kalisz would deliver her child, and that was precisely where Aleksandra was going.

Some minutes later, she had arrived at the hospital. She passed admittance and went straight to the maternity ward on the third floor. She was given a room right away. Aleksandra was so well known in the hospital that she often gave birth without seeing the doctor first.

"I feel that it's coming now," Aleksandra said.

"What do you mean?" asked the midwife. She looked tired.

"I'm going to give birth in a moment."

"Now? When did you start having contractions?"

"Not long ago, but I'm telling you that the child wants to be born – I feel it. It's my fourth child already."

The midwife looked at her rather snidely.

"And do you have any idea how many children I've delivered?"

She took out the routine questionnaire, which took a while to fill out.

"Now we'll give you a needle and wait for the little one."

But they didn't need to wait at all. The birth was imminent: the child literally "leapt" out. But … why wasn't the child crying? Aleksandra noticed that the little girl's umbilical cord had wrapped itself around her neck. She wasn't crying because she was unconscious.

"What's with the child?" Aleksandra asked with trepidation.

"Nothing, nothing – think of yourself," she heard.

Aleksandra cried out of anger and powerlessness. What had happened?

Her daughter was brought to her only after about two hours. Aleksandra was taken aback seeing an effusion of blood around the baby's eyes. What to do now?

She then recalled the Easter card that Uncle ("Uncle" was a nickname given to Fr. Wojtyła by his students) had sent her eight months earlier in which he wrote, "I'm praying for the life that is within you." She figured that if he was praying then, he would be now also.

Aleksandra finally saw her husband at the door – they had only now let him in.

"Leszek, it's not good," she said. Please give me some paper and a pen.

Her husband looked at her with sadness and took the paper and pen out of his pocket.

"We have a daughter but she was born with asphyxia. She's in critical condition. Please pray for her," she wrote.

"Please take this to Uncle and try to make sure he gets it quickly."

The following day, a friend of Aleksandra's brought her the reply:

"I celebrated Mass in your intention and hers. I entrust you to the Blessed Virgin, Mother of God."

Very soon after, they took the baby home from the hospital. With each day they were convincing themselves that the danger had passed. Some time later, they showed the child to Cardinal Wojtyła.

"She's beautiful," he said.

"Uncle, you helped save her."

Cardinal Wojtyła smiled.

"I prayed, I prayed," he said.

## "ALTHOUGH HE EXCHANGED HIS BANDANA FOR A PAPAL TIARA, UNCLE KEEPS ALL HIS OLD FRIENDS DEEP IN HIS HEART." *

Thirty years after these events, Aleksandra Ludwikowska is convinced that the prayers of then Cardinal Wojtyła helped heal her daughter, who today is a completely healthy adult woman.

When I spoke with her in her Cracow apartment, she apprised me of the great power of prayer that Father, then Bishop and later Cardinal Wojtyła had. What effect that prayer had on saving the life of the child some three decades ear-

---

* In Polish, this phrase forms a rhyming couplet and is part of a song composed by Father Wojtyła's canoeing companions.

lier is something that nobody can know with certainty. But among those who knew Pope John Paul II personally there is a strong conviction in the effectiveness of the prayers which he submitted to God.

Stanisław Rybicki met Karol Wojtyła in 1949 at St. Florian's Church in Cracow. He soon joined the academic youth ministry that the young priest was heading up and later would join on many outings with him. Finally, Stanisław married a young woman who also participated in the young-adult meetings. When I asked them about the prayers of Karol Wojtyła, they immediately gave examples from their own lives:

"It was autumn 1974," recalled Danuta Rybicka. "I left home to take my mother's lab test results to the hospital. My mother was to have an operation the next day because she had a cancerous growth under the lower eyelid. It was already evening and the weather was poor and rainy. I was walking by the Cracovia Hotel on my way to catch the streetcar. I saw a car coming with its headlights off and thought it could cause an accident and hit someone. That was the last thing I remembered. I lost consciousness, but think I may have regained it for a moment. I don't know if they took me to the hospital by ambulance or if I was already there. I felt that I was undressed and remembered thinking that I must be dying – and when was I last at confession? And then I lost consciousness again.

I was in a clinically dead state. Uncle wasn't in Cracow at the time, but he was informed of the accident right away. He had Mass in my intention and, upon his return to Poland, he came and visited me. I was in a body cast for eight months.

Later, I returned to work. The doctors couldn't believe that I could completely regain my health: that I could talk, walk and move normally, just as before the accident. For many years I continued to work as a teacher.

Stanisław Rybicki always kept the number to Archbishop Stanisław Dziwisz at the Vatican memorized in his mobile phone. It was the Archbishop who would convey information to the Holy Father, including a request for urgent prayer.

"I had a lump, a pericardial cyst, the doctors told me. They weren't certain whether it was malignant or benign," Stanisław recalled.

"It's significant since we asked for prayers and it turned out to be benign … but what happened in May 2002 is even more significant," his wife added. "My husband's breathing became irregular. We went to the hospital and had an x-ray done. It so happened that his lung had collapsed; he had to go to the hospital immediately for an operation. I ran to the hospital – John Paul II Hospital, interestingly. Normally it's hard to get in there, but they took my husband right away, which itself was a miracle. I next picked up the phone, called the Vatican and asked for prayers as my husband was very ill. The doctors were not sure at first how to treat him; one wanted to tap the lung while the other felt it was too great a risk.

"My lung had separated into two parts," Stanislaw recalled. "It was held together by the stitches from my previous operation. The doctors were attempting to decide whether to operate; they didn't want to take chances. I was 72 years old and they had already once opened my chest cavity. Finally they decided to at least tap the lung.

"I saw the x-ray and that the doctor was nervous. The nurse was holding my hand and trying to calm me, but I was terribly scared – I admit it, I was scared. I saw the doctor taking a large syringe into his hand. Fright still had me in its grip. Finally, the fear left me as I saw the doctor withdraw his hand. I glanced at the clock and thought, 'Oh, now I understand everything … this was the exact time when the Holy Father would pray. He always went down to the chapel before supper.' I calmed down completely. The doctor went about his work while the nurse talked to me. At one point I heard the question, 'does that hurt?' to which I answered 'yes, but only a little.' 'In that case thank God,' the doctor said. 'I think it's a miracle.' 'No, not a miracle,' I said, 'but my patron.' They took another x-ray and it turned out that the lung was normal, and in one piece."

"There were many such prayer requests to Uncle," recalled Danuta Rybicka.

"In 1992, Mietek Wisłocki, a doctor who used to go on canoe trips with us, had a stroke. It looked like a hopeless case. The Wisłockis have eight children living abroad; all of them came to say their final farewells to their father. Meanwhile, Uncle prayed for Mietek – and he was made well. Mietek was healthy for the next thirteen years. On March 20, 2005, however, Mietek again had a stroke. His wife Ewa called us and said, 'Staszek, I know that Uncle is very ill, but tell him that Mietek has had a stroke and is in critical condition." Stanisław called the Sisters of the Sacred Heart at the Papal residence. "We know that Uncle is very ill, but maybe the Sisters could at least pray for Mietek," he said. Not long after, the Holy Father died and we attended his funeral. One of the Sisters then told me: "Please tell Mrs. Wisłocka that the Holy Father celebrated Mass two days before his death in the intention of Dr. Wisłocki."

The Rybickis became emotional.

"Mietek lived through the stroke, although he's paralyzed," said Danuta Rybicka.

In August, on the day of Archbishop Dziwisz's inauguration, the Rybickis celebrated their 50th wedding anniversary.

"Although he exchanged his bandana for a Papal Tiara, Uncle keeps all his old friends deep in his heart," added Stanisław.

In Polish this was a rhyming couplet and part of a song dating back to the days of their canoe outings when Fr. Wojtyła would put a bandana on his head to protect against the sun. The Tiara, of course, is what Popes wear during ceremonies.

"Although he exchanged his bandana for a Papal Tiara,
Uncle keeps all his old friends deep in his heart."
Camping days reunion: John Paul II with friends,
their children and grandchildren.

*S*peaking of the miracles which Jesus performed during his earthly ministry, St. Au-
gustine, in an interesting text, interprets
them as signs of God's saving power and love and as incen-
tives to raise our minds to the kingdom of heavenly things.
"The miracles worked by our Lord Jesus Christ," St. Au-
gustine writes, "are divine works which raise the human
mind above visible things to understand what is divine" (In
Io. Ev. Tr., 24, 1).

Connected with this thought is the reaffirmation of the
close link of Jesus' "miracles-signs" with the call to faith.
These miracles demonstrate the existence of the supernatural order, which is the object of faith.

John Paul II
"Miracles Manifest the Supernatural Order"
General Audience, January 13, 1988

## BISHOP TADEUSZ PIERONEK

# THE POPE'S HEART WAS FILLED WITH GOD

At the entry to the building there is a short notice which reads that the Archdiocesan Museum, located there, was opened on September 28, 1978, by Cardinal Karol Wojtyła. That day went down in history as the day on which Pope John Paul I died at the Vatican. A few hours earlier, Cardinal Wojtyła celebrated the 20th anniversary of his ordination as Bishop. He then opened the museum. The next day he learned that he must travel to Rome to participate in his second conclave, the one at which he would be elected Pope.

Twenty seven years later, I met with Bishop Tadeusz Pieronek, a close collaborator of John Paul II and today the head of his beatification tribunal.

**When we were arranging to meet, Your Excellency, you said that you would answer those questions that you are permitted to answer. Can you tell us what questions we shouldn't ask?**

Questions regarding witnesses or when the tribunal will conclude, as this isn't foreseeable. Nor can I say what questions will be asked, as these are determined by the tribunal in Rome. If I feel it to be appropriate, I can add another question. In general I can say that the questions will concern behaviour, pronouncements and various situations that attest to the extraordinary nature of the person. There are many other confidential aspects that will emerge in the course of the tribunal.

**Isn't the whole process somewhat for show, though? Everyone already knows that John Paul II will be canonized.**

The procedure itself is required because all candidates for beatification and sainthood go through it. Why should one person be exempt? Of course, he was the Pope and an extraordinary person, and the whole world acknowledges it. Because of this, the five-year waiting period for the commencement of the beatification process has been waived and will probably be shortened along the way.

At the same time, we cannot go by arguments of the type that everyone already knows or that popular opinion has already deemed John Paul II a saint. Certain formalities must be observed. Indeed, looking back over ten centuries throughout Church history, that is the way that saints have been proclaimed. In each case, it is the people's will ratified by the Bishop. It isn't a meaningless tradition in the Church. After all, if it was important during the time of John Paul II himself then surely it must mean something. I think it indicates an awareness of the Church that it is to do this, also in light of the requirements of sainthood in the world today. And if this comes about spontaneously, it is a sign of the liveliness of the Church in today's society.

**Today, "Santo subito" has become somewhat of a slogan. Why is the beatification of John Paul II so urgent?**

Because people are seeking it. And, they believe that procedures should yield to higher reasons.

**What reasons are those?**

The faithful believe that John Paul II should be declared a saint. We have to remember that the Church is not just the bishops and the Pope; the Church is all of God's people: the Pope, bishops, priests and faithful all taken as a whole. It isn't 'we the clergy' and 'you the people.'

So if the Church, taken as such, is saying 'People, hurry up – this is too important to wait around,' then we definitely feel the importance of having an advocate and of living like he did and giving a similar example by means of our lives, since this is connected to God's promise to us of a life together with Him.

**Of what significance to the beatification process are the testimonies of extraordinary happenings that occurred through the Pope's intercession during his lifetime?**

The crux of the issue is that he was a Pope for the people and that something simply radiated from his person. Personally, I am convinced that extraordinary happenings did take place, but I also feel that normal human reactions may have played a role in the various circumstances through people simply meeting the Pope. It's not often that people meet with the Pope. We can even take the example of children who see some television personality live: to them it's as if they're in heaven. It may manifest itself through a release of interior tension and through joy. The meetings with the Pope were of a similar nature and very often they were key events in the lives of people who came to them with expectations. They came and were not let down: the Holy Father was touchable, open, understanding and well-wishing. He was not afraid to come into contact with dirty people, sinners … People want to be treated seriously, to see that someone cares about them and treats them with love. So from a psychological standpoint, these meetings could have been characterized by bliss, ease, and joy and nurtured that which was in the person which later emerged and for which they prepared themselves, or for which God prepared them.

**But it also happened that people did not get to see the Pope yet something changed in their lives; their health improved when the Pope prayed for them.**

A miracle in Christianity is predicated on the religious person praying to God through the intercession of an individual, which proves effective, and the person believes it to have been so. The Church, however, has tighter criteria for defining miracles and may not identify a given event as such. But there is nothing wrong with people subjectively treating such occurrences as miraculous interventions by God.

**Will John Paul II's prayer life be discussed during the beatification tribunal? Many have believed in its effectiveness.**

Most likely so, if the witnesses choose to mention it.

**Is it significant that the Pope prayed for people's requests and that later those very requests were answered?**

It is. As far as I know the Pope always prayed that God's will be done. That is, after all, the only logical form of prayer. We can't force God to believe that He's wrong and that we want things to conform to our expectations; we need to ask Him that His will for us take place. Such is the thinking of a person who knows who he is in relation to God; a person who believes that on the other side is a Being who doesn't want to cause us grief but who wants the best for us in any given moment.

**But the Holy Father often prayed for specific requests...**

In the way I've just described. As far as I am aware, he always prayed that God do that which He deems to be best.

**Can we speak of the extraordinary nature of Karol Wojtyła's prayers?**

I'm not a judge in the matter. I can speak at best as a witness. I have never met a person who could pray so discreetly, so often and so deeply. It wasn't always overt, but there were moments when his prayer was plainly visible – for example, at Wawel during his last pilgrimage. The Holy Father prayed over his breviary for over half an hour. The world saw that

107

he treasured God above all. It wasn't that the crowds were cheering all over the place and he was ignoring them; it was that he gave an example of what takes priority in life. For him, God was always that priority. The Pope could pray for half an hour at Wawel and later half an hour at Kalwaria. In so doing he showed what his mission was all about.

**By that time he was Pope. Did such moments of prayer occur before then too?**

He always retreated into prayer and did it with discretion in such a way as not to draw attention to himself. He never said, "excuse me, I'm going to pray," as he was in fact constantly praying. He would be in a deep state of thought (praying above all else, I assume), and we would sometimes have to interrupt him. But he never said anything like 'Don't disturb me, I'm praying.' He always had time for anyone who turned to him. He was also able to create the sort of atmosphere that would let you know that it's best to give him the time he needs in prayer and not bother him with banal things - there'd be time for that later. One knew it was best to give him time to do what was important to him: prayer and personal reflection.

**Did it ever make you wonder why the one in charge was praying while there was something important that needed to be done?**

Yes. In Italy … we were in Etna one time returning to Catania, from where we were to catch the flight to Rome. He sat down on a stone ledge next to the road, took out his breviary and began to pray. Both the priest who was driving that day and I knew that we might not make the flight because we would have to drive across the entire city of Catania where road construction had been taking place, slowing the traffic even more. The traffic was comparable to that which we have in the large cities in Poland today. This, coupled with the fact that the airport was on the other side of town, would make it extremely difficult to get there on time. So we told him that there's very little time and we have to get going. But this didn't faze him at all; he kept on praying until he got through his breviary, then he got into the car and we drove

John Paul II prays at the Wawel Cathedral, Cracow, Poland. August 18, 2002.

off. We got to the airport half an hour late, just as we knew we would. However, the plane hadn't yet departed. Why? In the morning we had visited the Archbishop of Catania, who was also returning to Rome for the Synod. I assume that it was thanks to him that the plane hadn't left since he probably mentioned that the Archbishop of Cracow would be on the flight as well.

**Will testimonies like this – Karol Wojtyła's emphasizing prayer more than getting to the airport on time – also figure into the beatification process?**

Certainly so, because it's a question of his disposition to prayer, which was extraordinary. Those who were close to him know how much time he spent in prayer – hours and hours – and this was taking into account the enormous responsibilities he had to the Universal Church. Still, he never neglected prayer.

**Did he pray at night too?**

I don't know about that, but he would get up early after retiring at a late hour. He didn't need much sleep.

**We've heard people speak about the 'magnetism' of John Paul II. Was this part of his strong personality or was there something else?**

It was something else. He wasn't a psychotherapist or healer like some who come from abroad and lay their hands on people's heads. He didn't consider himself a healer. His heart was filled with God, and that was enough for him.

**In the case of extraordinary events attributed to the Pope's intercession, medicine did play a part in the outcomes, but people believed that the prayers of John Paul II were what healed them. What's the relationship between the natural and supernatural here?**

Medicine is getting ever more advanced and effective. Some of today's medical achievements could have saved millions of lives in the past. Back then we didn't have all the things we have today. In the future we are sure to have even better means of fighting disease. However, there are limits to what medicine can do, and in such circumstances we see God's intervention.

**The Pope himself said that the lives of the saints, Church history, but above all else the investigations into the lives of God's servants make up the "documentation" which, when analyzed rigorously in view of history and medicine, will prove the existence of the 'Power from on high' that supersedes the natural order and works within it. What will be rigorously analyzed during the beatification tribunal of John Paul II?**

If there are any extraordinary occurrences, they will be analyzed, physical healings especially. But of greater importance are the spiritual healings – conversions; but these are more difficult to document. Physicians are able to ascertain physical healings. Usually the people who were healed sought medical help for years beforehand and documentation to that effect is plentiful. The doctors finally conclude that given the circumstances, the turnaround in the condition of the patient was literally impossible. That is their task. Someone else will then say, "It did happen, and it happened because of God's contact with that person." The Church then accepts it as a case of supernatural intervention of God.

I think that if we talk about miracles occurring today, we can look to the characteristics of miracles that happened in the Acts of the Apostles. We recall the scene where Peter, upon entering the sanctuary, finds a beggar asking for money. The Apostle answers him by saying, "I have neither silver nor gold, but what I do have I give you: in the name of Jesus Christ the Nazarean, rise and walk." (Acts 3:6)

*I do not like the term "crowd," which bears a sense of anonimity. I prefer the term "multi-tude" (in Greek: "plethos": Mark 3:7 ; Luke 6:17 ; Acts 2:6 ; 5:15, etc.) Jesus walked along the roads of Palestine and the multitudes often followed him; so it was with the Apostles. Of course, in my ministry it is necessary that I meet with many people - sometimes with the multi-tudes.*

John Paul II
*Rise, Let Us Be On Our Way*

# Chapter 4.

## THE SPIRIT BREATHES

During the weekly general audiences throughout his pontificate, Pope John Paul II met with almost 18 million people – 17,600,000 to be exact. Millions more are added to that when one takes into account those participating in his international gatherings and trips across Italy.

From the earliest hours of his pontificate it was clear that the Polish Pope did not see himself as a prisoner of the Vatican – he wanted to go out to the people and invite them to him. Already before his official inauguration, John Paul II broke with tradition by visiting Gemelli Hospital to see an ailing friend, Bishop (today Cardinal) Andrzej Deskur. Less than three months after his election to the Papacy, John Paul II made his first international pilgrimage to Mexico. Millions lined the streets along which he passed. In *Rise, Let Us Be On Our Way*, John Paul II recalled that one could literally feel the faith of the countless who gathered.

Six months later, he was in Poland. First, he met with some 300,000 people at Victory Square (today Pilsudski Square) in Warsaw, and then with a million people in Jasna Góra, and finally with two-and-a-half million at Błonie park in Cracow.

Not only in his native Poland and in Mexico did the Pope draw such enormous numbers of faithful: in 1995, almost five million people gathered for Mass in Manila, the capital city of the Philippines – it was the largest Mass in human history and possibly the largest one-time gathering of people ever in one location. In 1997, over a million people took part in the concluding ceremonies of World Youth Day in Paris. This was a huge surprise in a country as secularized as France: the organizers were expecting a mere 300,000 participants. The Jubilee Year celebrations in 2000 drew eight million people to Rome, of which over two million were youth who met with the Holy Father at Tor Vergata in August 2000.

John Paul II saw these immense gatherings as near-repetitions of what we read in Acts 2:1-6 : When the time for Pentecost was fulfilled, they were all in one place together. And suddenly there came from the sky a noise like a strong driving wind, and it filled the entire house in which they were. Then there appeared to them tongues as of fire, which parted and came to rest on each one of them. And they were all filled with the Holy Spirit and began to speak in different

Vatican, April 8, 2005

tongues, as the Spirit enabled them to proclaim. Now there were devout Jews from every nation under heaven staying in Jerusalem. At this sound, they gathered in a large crowd, but they were confused because each one heard them speaking in his own language.

Another great crowd gathered around John Paul II one last time on April 8, 2005. Not only pilgrims from around the world attended the funeral of the Pope from Poland in great numbers – thanks to the worldwide reach of television, over a billion people were able to follow the funeral. We saw the cypress coffin on the ground and the Holy Gospel placed on top of it. The wind tossed about the Cardinals' and Bishops' vestments and lifted their skullcaps off their heads; it also caused the pages of the open Gospel to flip about. This didn't seem out of the ordinary since the sheets themselves are light. Later, though, the wind turned over the much heavier cover - closing those pages that had previously been open. The Book was now closed. Many of the media personnel present could not help but notice the breath of the Spirit.

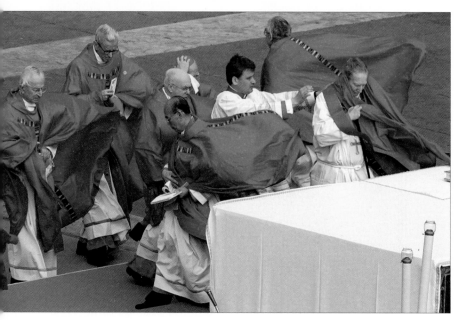

Vatican, April 8, 2005

Pope John Paul II at Victory Square, Warsaw, Poland.
June 2, 1979.

*And I, son of this Polish earth and at the same time Pope John Paul II, cry from the depths of this millenium on the eve of Pentecost:*

*Send forth Your Spirit!*

*Send forth Your Spirit!*

*And renew the face of the earth.*

*This earth!*

*Amen.*

John Paul II
Warsaw, Victory Square, June 2, 1979

# SEND FORTH YOUR SPIRIT

Mrs. Feliksa quickened her steps to the point that her children were barely able to keep up with her. It was already pretty late and she was on her way to Victory Square, where John Paul II was going to say the first Mass during his trip to Poland. Even though it was late afternoon, it was still very hot and Mrs. Feliksa could feel the sweat dripping down her back. They finally got to Królewski Street, and after passing some metal barriers they went in the direction of the Hotel Victoria. People kept arriving and it began to get crowded. She made the decision to stop, especially since she noticed a free space by the barrier separating the sidewalk from the road. "Maybe the Pope will drive by here and I will see him from close up?" she thought. She saw a huge wooden cross with a gigantic stole hanging from it. The cross stood behind the altar put up opposite the Saski Garden and the Tomb of the Unknown Soldier in the direction of the square.

She was glad that she came. It was a change of pace from her hard, not to say sad, life. Eighteen years earlier she had married. Not long after the wedding she discovered that her husband had a bad habit: he drank excessively. Some nights, he would not come home at all. When he did come home he would swear so much that it hurt her ears. Feeling helpless, she wondered how long she could put up with it. She felt sorry for her children that they had to see their father like this.

118

The atmosphere at the square helped her forget about her daily life. When she saw the Pope in his somewhat strange yet familiar popemobile, constructed from the undercarriage of a Polish truck, she really felt good. It so happened that John Paul II really did pass by very close to her. He even looked at her and blessed her.

"I somehow felt lighter," recalled Mrs. Feliksa. "And I remember what he said: 'Send forth Your spirit and renew the face of the earth.' I only regret that I didn't go to communion that time. You see, I wasn't practising my faith regularly then."

We are talking beside the same cross that stood at Victory Square on June 2, 1979. Today the cross stands next to Mrs. Feliksa's parish.

"At that time in 1979 did you believe that something in your life could change?" I asked.

"No."

Today everything is different: Mrs. Feliksa refers to that cross as her own.


"A couple of years ago, Father Paul Rossa, who worked in our parish, got an idea to decorate this cross with a stole, just like the one that hung on it in Victory Square," recalled an older woman.

"The youth in our parish were going to receive the Sacrament of Confirmation," explained Father Rossa (who now works in Ukraine), "and last year it so happened that June 2-3 fell on Saturday and Sunday, just like when the Pope came to Poland. I thought it was a good occasion to remember that day by hanging a new stole on the cross (following that Papal Mass, the cross stood on the grounds of our parish). I never realized how much difficulty I'd have trying to make the stole. I had to run around to find the material and then I had to find someone to sew it together."

"My friend who spent more time in church than I did knew that I sewed," said Mrs Feliksa. "She came to me and asked me if I would do this. I was delighted that I'd be able to decorate my cross."

"Why do you call it 'yours'?"

She smiled uneasily. She had spoken freely about the stole, but now it became harder for her.

"You see, I used to come here for a long time," she said. "In the evening, when no one could see, I knelt and I leaned my head, here" – she touched the cross – "and I prayed. In fact I cried because I didn't really know how to pray."

"In 1981 she had been married for twelve years, twelve years of suffering due to her husband's alcoholism. Nothing had changed; in fact it was getting worse. In the mid-1980s she met a lawyer to whom she told her troubles. According to the lawyer the solution was simple: to continue this way was absurd. It would be better to file for divorce and evict her alcoholic husband from the apartment. She convinced Mrs. Feliksa to take the matter to court.

"But I started to think that maybe I shouldn't do that. By title, it was actually my husband's apartment and now I was going to throw him out?" she said. "That's when I began coming here to pray. When he was not home at night, I would come to the Papal cross. I later arranged for a Mass to be said at Licheń."

She took a slightly yellowed prayer card out bearing an image of Christ crucified; on the other side was confirmation that thirty Masses had been said in the intention of healing her addicted husband from alcoholism. "I didn't send much money, yet they gave me thirty Masses!" she smiled uneasily.

"I don't know how it happened, but my husband started to drink less and less. Finally he stopped altogether. He stopped smoking too and he doesn't even swear anymore," she said, smiling happily.

"Do you still come to pray under this cross?"

"Of course."

120

Mass at Victory Square, Warsaw, Poland, June 2, 1979.

On Saturday April 2, 2005, she was there at nine o'clock in the evening. Under the cross there burned hundreds of candles and people were praying for John Paul II. She returned home and half an hour later she heard that the Pope had returned to the house of the Father. From that time, Mrs. Feliksa goes there regularly in the evening of the second day of each month to pray.

"I pray for his beatification, but I also pray to him," she says.

"In August they found out that Mrs. Feliksa's husband was sick with cancer.

"It has spread to other parts of his body," she sighed. "But he will live awhile," she added with a deep sense of optimism.

Mass at Victory Square, Warsaw, Poland, June 2, 1979.

*I* s my pilgrimage to my native land, in the year in which the Church in Poland marks the 900th anniversary of the death of Saint Stanislaus, not perhaps a particular sign of our Polish pilgrimage through the history of the Church, not only in the history of our native land but also that of Europe and the world? I set aside my person here, yet I must ask – we all must ask – why after many centuries of tradition, a son of the Polish Nation, of the Polish earth, has been called to the chair of Saint Peter in Rome. Christ demanded of Peter and of the other Apostles that they be His witnesses "in Jerusalem, in all of Judea and Samaria, and to the ends of the earth" (Acts 1,8). With reference, therefore, to these words of Christ, do we not have the right to think that in our times, perhaps Poland has been given the responsibility of bearing this witness?

Yet, if we accept everything that I have dared to assert in this moment, how many great duties and obligations are suddenly required of us! Are we ready for this challenge?

John Paul II
Victory Square, Warsaw. June 2, 1979.

# TWO RELICS

When this account took place, the author of this paragraph heard and saw John Paul II live for the first time. As an eighteen-year-old young man, I went to Victory Square because I saw that something important was happening. I never imagined that I would partake in an historical event. I did not know that in the same crowd was a woman who was suffering from her husband's addiction. I did not know that Cardinal Wyszyński, standing next to the Pope, was wondering about – how did he put it? – "the strange verdicts of Divine Providence". The Cardinal later related how participating in the Papal Mass made him remember a different time when he used to walk this way as a boy and would see the huge Orthodox church put up by the czar of Russia as a sign of Russian domination over Poland.

After a little while it became clear that the famous words "Send forth Your Spirit" were a public prayer and expression of the Pope's faith as he authentically asked God to "renew the face of the earth". If someone had then said that in a year and a half Poland would have a labour union registered as officially independent of the Communist power, the average Pole would have thought that person to be crazy. If someone had said that in nine years the system created in Yalta would collapse and that the Berlin Wall would be taken down, people would call him ... a believer in miracles. But that is exactly what happened.

I think that John Paul II deeply believed in "the breath of the Spirit" which first renewed the face of Poland and then the rest of Europe. It just so happened that the beginning of the Pope's pilgrimage to his native land began a day before the feast of Pentecost. The following day the Pope was in Gniezno where the phrase "the two lungs of Europe" was first uttered. A week later on Sunday June 10 on the greens of Cracow he confirmed events, telling his fellow countrymen: "You have to be strong ..."

Twelve years later when the Pope was in Gniezno, he again recalled that pilgrimage and the homily he had given in the first capital of Poland on June 3, 1979:

"From this place a huge wave of the Holy Spirit has poured out. Here the thought of a new evangelization began to assume a concrete form. In this time great changes took place, new chances arose, and new people appeared. The wall separating Europe collapsed. Fifty years after the beginning of World War II the consequences stopped eroding the face of our continent. The half-century of separation ended, especially for the millions of inhabitants of Central and Eastern Europe who had paid a terrible price for it."

In the eyes of the Pope, that which happened between 1979 and 1989 had the mark of the "Power from on high."

Two physical signs – one might say *relics* – are connected to these events.

One of these is the cross from Victory Square. It was taken down a few hours after that Mass. The fear of the authorities was so great that they quickly took down the cross during the night between June 2-3. Today the cross can be found next to St. Maximilian Kolbe Parish in Warsaw's Służewic district. During martial law, illegal underground publications were concealed inside the cross. Twelve years after the famous Papal Mass the cross was once again taken to Victory Square. On June 13, 1999, John Paul II celebrated Mass there, during which he beatified 108 martyrs of the Second World War.

The second sign is the bullet that hit the Pope on May 13, 1981. The bullet is now at Fatima. It is well known that the Pope connected his miraculous survival with the revelations of Fatima. He also linked the fall of communism and the end of the system created at Yalta with these revelations. Two pieces of the Berlin Wall are clear reminders of this. One of these can be found at Fatima, and the other in the gardens of the Vatican, where John Paul II would often walk and pray.

Half a century of separation is ended.
The wall that separates Europe collapses.

"I EXPERIENCED
A DEADLY THREAT TO MY LIFE
AND GREAT SUFFERING,
WHILE AT THE SAME TIME
THE GREAT MERCY
OF GOD.
THROUGH THE INTERCESSION
OF OUR LADY OF FATIMA,
I REGAINED MY LIFE."

# SAVED

"Where?"

"In the stomach."

"Does is it hurt very much?"

"Yes. O Mary, my Mother! Mary, my Mother!"

This is how Archbishop Stanisław Dziwisz described the short exchange of words between himself and John Paul II shortly after the Pope was shot by Mehmet Ali Agca.

Writer André Frossard has described the sequence of events that followed as without a doubt miraculous. A simple coincidence of events is not enough to explain all the facts.

The would-be assassin assumed that John Paul II was wearing a bullet-proof vest: this is why he did not aim for the heart, but at the stomach instead. The Pope moved his hand at the moment when the assassin fired; the bullet struck his finger and changed its course by a millimetre, and because of this it missed an artery. Had it struck that artery, he would have bled to death in minutes. After two shots Ali Agca's gun jammed. They drove the Pope to the ambulance which he had blessed the day before, saying "May it never be needed." The ambulance had been donated to the Vatican and was kept nearby in case a pilgrim needed assistance. It reached the Gemelli clinic in eight minutes, even though it usually takes forty minutes given the traffic at that time of day. What was even more amazing was the fact that they got there so fast without a siren; it had broken down. And then, of course,

there was the operation. The clinic personnel were waiting for the Pope knowing that something had happened, but they didn't know what. Professor Tresalti, who happened to be at the hospital, heard the word "Colpito!" which in Italian means stricken, wounded or hit. It could have been a heart attack, a stroke, or some kind of an accident. The Pope was first taken to the ninth floor where a room was prepared for him, and then to the operating room. Precious time ebbed away. Worse yet, the most experienced surgeon, Professor Francesco Crucitti, was not there nor was he at home. There were no cellular phones in those days.

Professor Crucitti looked up to see a very distraught nun in the doorway; he had been visiting a patient at the clinic on via Aurelia.

"Professor! The Holy Father!" she called out.

"There was an attempt on his life! They shot him!"

Crucitti stared at her stunned. "No, this is impossible!" he thought.

"Where is the phone?" he asked.

The sister took him to the phone. The professor dialed the number to Gemelli. One, two, three rings ... Nobody was answering!

He quickly changed and put on his jacket. In no time at all he was in his car.

Traffic jams! Rome's traffic jams! Crucitti decided on a make-or-break manoeuvre. He got into the left lane, put his hand on the horn and joined a convoy of speeding police cars with their sirens blaring. A moment later he saw a policeman on motorcycle chasing him in his rear-view mirror. Crucitti was convinced that the policeman would stop him and give him a ticket. When the motorcycle pulled up by the car, the professor yelled out in desperation:

"I have to be at Gemelli immediately!"

The policeman understood. He sped up and made way for Crucitti.

Within a few minutes they were at the entrance of the hospital.

In the operating room the team literally tore off Crucitti's clothes. In a few seconds he had his operation uniform on. He washed his hands as they put on his overall and his shoes. The doctor came to him.

"Pressure 80, 70 and falling," he said.

They entered the room. Dr. Crucitti leaned over the Pope.

He saw blood. A lot of blood. They began to drain the abdominal cavity. After a moment they were able to see the damage. Dr. Crucitti stopped the bleeding.

The blood pressure slowly began to rise.

Crucitti saw many wounds in the abdominal cavity. One was created by the bullet, others by bursting. The worst injury was at the rear of the colon. However, no vital organ had been disturbed: the bullet only brushed the organs that if damaged could have meant death. A half-hour before midnight the last stitches were put in. Already on May 14, at fifteen minutes to one o'clock in the morning, a statement was issued that the operation had been successful.

"When I fell in St Peter's Square I had a distinct feeling that I would recover," said the Pope to André Frossard. "This certainty never left me, whether at the time when it was at its worst following the first operation or when I was sick with the virus afterwards. Someone's hand had shot me, but Another Hand directed the bullet," added the Holy Father.

Arturo Mari related his conversation with Professor Crucitti:

"The bullet, said the professor as he was showing me the film, momentarily changed direction as if it came up against a piece of steel. This is unthinkable because inside the body the parts are soft; there aren't even any bones. How this happened only our most Blessed Virgin Mary knows."

Father Dziwisz describes the path of the bullet like this:

"It passed the main artery by millimetres; had the artery been damaged it would have meant certain death. It did not touch the spine or any other vital point. Between us I can say that this was miraculous. As for the rest, I give credit to the super speed with which they brought the Holy Father to the hospital, the presence of the doctors who operated magnificently, I repeat, magnificently."

It is worth paying attention to these words of the Pope's closest co-worker.

"The Holy Father saw in all of this a sign from heaven and we, together with the doctors, saw a miracle," said Father Dziwisz.

This miracle, however, differed from those known healings where an ailment disappears in some mysterious way and people recover their health despite the doctors having said there was no hope for them. The most amazing such example was described by Vittorio Messori: "El milagro de los milagros" – "Miracle of miracles" – which occurred in the 17th century in Spain. One night, a peasant named Miguel Juan had a leg grow back (historians wrote that it was "restored") that had been amputated many years earlier. This miracle was precisely documented and accepted by Church authorities.

In John Paul II's case, it was different. The best professionals had to rise to an incredible challenge and put in their best performance. Thus the individuals were actively involved, but those who were witness to these events were convinced that they were not acting alone. "It seemed to everyone that an invisible hand was directing everything," said Father Dziwisz. "We did not talk of a miracle, but we were all thinking of it as such."

What was even more interesting was the fact that the confirmation of this extraordinary event went relatively unnoticed.

"The injured finger began to heal on its own," answered the Holy Father's secretary following the attempt on his life. "During the operation no one really paid too much attention to it. The doctors had planned to amputate it. Meanwhile an

Visible in the foreground is the injury to the Holy Father's finger - doctors had planned amputation, but despite the shattered joint the finger returned to a completely normal condition on its own.

ordinary splint and the medicine given to help him regain his overall health were enough to heal the finger. Notwithstanding this, the second joint had been totally destroyed ... Now the finger is completely healed and functional."

On June 3, the Pope returned to the Vatican. He was not completely well yet: he was feeling the effects of his wounds. His tooth had been broken during the application of anaesthesia ,but that wasn't the worst of it. Shortly thereafter, John Paul II was attacked by an enemy worse, perhaps, than Ali Agca: the Pope contracted a cytomegalovirus from the blood transfusion he had received and had to return to the hospital. During this second stay at the hospital, John Paul II asked that a sealed document from the Congregation for the Doctrine of the Faith known as *The Secret of Fatima* be brought to him. The Pope pointed out that the attempt on his life occurred on the same day and the same hour as the first appearance of the Virgin Mary in Fatima in 1917. The message from Fatima was made known in the form of two secrets. There was a third secret which had not been disclosed; the only ones allowed knowledge of it were the Pope and the Prefect of the Congregation for the Doctrine of the Faith. Earlier, Popes John XXIII and Paul VI had each read the message and decided not to reveal its contents. The Polish Pope acquainted himself with the text only in 1981, two and half years after he was elected to the chair of St. Peter. On July 18, the then Prefect of the Congregation for the Doctrine of the Faith, Cardinal Franjo Seper, gave the Archbishop Eduardo Martinez Somalo, the substitute of Secretariat of State, two envelopes: a white one with the original text in Portuguese from Sister Lucia and an orange one bearing the Italian translation. On August 11, both envelopes were returned to the archives.

What did John Paul II read in them?

*In the immense light that is God, we saw "something similar to how people appear in a mirror when they pass in front of it," a Bishop dressed in white, "we had the impression that it was the Holy Father". We saw other Bishops, Priests, men and women religious going up a steep mountain, at the*

136

John Paul II before the statue of Our Lady of Fatima. May 2000.

*top of which there was a big Cross of rough-hewn trunks as of a cork tree with its bark; before reaching there the Holy Father passed through a big city half in ruins and half trembling, with halting step, afflicted with pain and sorrow, he prayed for the souls of the corpses he met on his way; having reached the top of the mountain, on his knees at the foot of the big Cross he was killed by a group of soldiers....*

But the Pope survived.

Three years later – in March 1984 – the Bishop of Fatima, Alberto Amaral, came to Rome. He brought with him a statue of the Virgin Mary. At first the statue stood in the Pope's private apartment. The Holy Father spent the night of March 24-25 in prayer in front of the statue. The following day John Paul II did something that he had been planning for a long time. It was directly connected to the apparition that three children, Lucia, Francesco and Jacinta, witnessed in Fatima on July 13, 1917, and was described in the first two secrets of the Fatima:

Our Lady showed us a great sea of fire which seemed to be under the earth. Plunged in this fire were demons and souls in human form like transparent burning embers, all blackened or burnished bronze, floating about in the conflagration, now raised into the air by the flames that issued from within themselves together with great clouds of smoke, then falling back on every side like sparks in a huge fire without weight or equilibrium and amid shrieks and groans of pain and despair which horrified and made us tremble.

This was the first part of the famous secrets of Fatima. Mary told the children that the war would soon end; however, if people do not cease offending God, a worse one will break out during the Pontificate of Pius XI ...To prevent this, I shall come to ask for the consecration of Russia to my Immaculate Heart, and the Communion of reparation on the First Saturdays. If my requests are heeded Russia will be converted, and there will be peace; if not, she will spread her errors throughout the world, causing wars and persecutions of the Church. This is the second part of the secret. Only the Pope and a few people close to him knew about the third part.

After the assassination attempt on May 13, 1981, John Paul II prepared himself to answer the request mentioned in the second part of the apparition. On March 25 in St. Peter's Square, the Pope said: "Mother of all individuals and peoples ... accept our cry ... and embrace with love, Mother and Handmaid of the Lord this human world of ours which we entrust and consecrate to you, for we are full of concern for the earthly and eternal destiny of individuals and peoples. In a special way we entrust and consecrate to you those individuals and nations which especially need to be entrusted and consecrated."

Before leaving Rome, Bishop Amaral once again visited the Pope. John Paul II presented him with a small box.

"This is the bullet taken out of my body on May 13, 1981," he said. "The second one was lost somewhere in St. Peter's Square. It doesn't belong to me, but to the One who took care of me and saved me. I want you to take it to Fatima and put it in the sanctuary as a sign of my gratitude to the Most Blessed Virgin and as a witness to great deeds of God.

## GOD WILL KEEP HIS WORD

"Father, do you think you could place the bullet in the crown of the statue?" suggested Bishop Amaral to the Rector of Fatima. The Bishop had returned from Rome and was trying to decide what to do with the Papal gift.

"I don't know how to do that," replied Father Luciano Guerra.

The bullet really didn't match the decorations on the crown ... How could a piece of lead match a masterpiece of golden art, embellished with 313 pearls and almost 3,000 priceless gems? The crown was made according to a model of the royal crown: it has eight closed hoops and a globe made of turquoise symbolizing the world. At its base, the hoops meet forming a small hole. Father Guerra thought for a minute. He took the bullet and placed it up to that hole – it fit perfectly!

Not long after these events the Apostolic Nuncio of Portugal met with Sister Lucia.

"Has Russia now been consecrated?" he asked her.

"Yes, it now has," she replied.

"So we are waiting for a miracle."

"God will keep His word," said Sister Lucia.

Four years later Poland was overtaken by a wave of strikes.

In January 1989, once again, Solidarity was legalized. Talks began at a round table in February during which the authorities met with the opposition. These talks led to the establishment of a date for the first partially free elections in Poland since before the war. The elections turned out to be an absolute victory for Solidarity. In August, John Paul II travelled to Santiago de Compostella in Spain, where he led World Youth Day. On August 23 the Pope, back in Rome, summarized the youth gathering, calling the sanctuary "a privileged place, where the light of Christianity shines upon Europe as from a lantern – on Old Europe, which finds itself on the eve of unity in the face of Christianity's third millennium."

The next day, Wojciech Jaruzelski asked Tadeusz Mazowiecki to form a new government. On September 12 the first non-communist premier since the end of World War II began his term in office. On the evening of November 8-9 the Berlin Wall collapsed.

The Pope travelled to Fatima on three separate occasions.
His last visit took place May 12-13, 2000, when the publication
of the Third Secret of Fatima was announced. In this picture:
The Holy Father places a ring given to him by Cardinal Stefan
Wyszynski at the feet of the statue of Our Lady of Fatima,
Mother of God.

# manila '95

X Giornata
Mondiale
della Gioventù

X World
Youth
Day

Xème Journée
Mondiale
de la Jeunesse

X Jornada
Mundial
de la Juventud

*O*f course the mission I fulfill demands that I meet with many people, sometimes with great numbers of people. It was like this in Manila, for example, where there were millions of young people. However, one cannot speak of an anonymous crowd, neither there nor in any other place.

In Manila, I had all of Asia before my eyes. So many Christians ... yet at the same time, so many who still do not know Christ! I place great hope in the dynamism of the Church in the Philippines and Korea. Asia: our mutual assignment for the Third Millennium!

John Paul II,
*Rise, Let Us Be On Our Way*

# PHILIPPINE
# MIRACLES

Already from the helicopter window the Pope could see the incredible sight. On the horizon, the South China Sea, its eastern end jutting far inland creating a vast gulf; on land, another sea – a sea of people who had filled in every available space. He had already been there the night before. The biggest park in the Philippine capital, Manila, was illuminated by hundreds of thousands of candles. If that scene had inspired awe in him, what could he think today? In the morning the pilgrimage organizers had told him that he would not be able to travel to the site by popemobile because the roads were completely blocked by people. The helicopter circled the bay and landed at Quirino Stand, near the Papal altar. Not long after this John Paul II appeared at the door of the helicopter. With the help of a cane he walked the few steps down to the ground. He moved past the welcoming crowd and made his way to the makeshift sacristy in order to prepare for Mass.

It was January 15, 1995, a Sunday – a day which passed into history as likely having seen the biggest gathering of people in one place in all time.

"We had to go through the crowd and make a way for ourselves in order to see the Holy Father," recalled Michel Remery of Holland. "There were so many people that moving over ten centimetres in any direction was extremely difficult. Yet move they did." Remery was sent as a delegate from Holland to the World Youth Day in Manila. He found himself there somewhat by accident. A priest had asked him if he

Mass concluding the 10th World Youth Day in Manila. January 15, 1995.

THE EXPONENT OF PHILIPPINE PROGRESS SINCE 1900

# MANILA BULLETIN

## THE NATION'S LEADING NEWSPAPER

LET US UNITE THE NATION AND MOVE FORWARD

VOL. 265 No. 15 ★ ★ ★ MONDAY MORNING, JANUARY 16, 1995 60 PAGES — P6.00 IN METRO MANILA

## Largest crowd at Luneta

The last time Filipinos took to the streets in such large numbers they were overthrowing a tyrant, but yesterday they were drawn by a septuagenarian Pole with a message of hope and love.

Pope John Paul II encountered what Vatican officials said were clearly the largest crowds of his 17-year reign when he brought his five-day visit to the Philippines to a triumphant climax with a mass at the Luneta to mark World Youth Day.

Police and Vatican officials put the crowd at more than four million, dwarfing the million or so who faced down tanks and guns in the 1986 "people power" revolution that ejected President Ferdinand Marcos from 20 corrupt years in power.

The Philippines, Asia's only mainly Christian country, has given the 74-year-old Polish Pontiff a rapturous welcome since he ar-

(Turn to page 26, col. 1)

wanted to participate in a gathering that was to take place in the Philippines. He thought it was an interesting proposition due to the exotic location and the chance to meet other young people from all over the world.

"In childhood I was baptized a Catholic and I was raised a Catholic, but to be honest I didn't differ much from the other students in Holland," he said. "I lived as they lived. Religious matters did not interest me much. Whenever I went into a Church I saw old people with grey hair listening to the priest talk about something that didn't have anything to do with me. For example, the priest would say: 'Too bad our grandchildren are not here, too bad that the churches are not full.' I thought to myself, 'But I am here, so tell me something about this Jesus I want to get to know.' I had no luck finding Jesus in the Church, so I thought that even though Jesus' message is good it didn't look like the Church was still alive; I thought it had died."

In the Philippines Remery saw something else.

The first days following his arrival, coupled with the youth vigil on Saturday, January 14, made a deep impression on him. He had never seen so many young people - singing, happy, responding with such life to the words of John Paul II. He looked at the Pope with surprise. His invalid state notwithstanding, the Pope joined in the dancing and the singing of the young people.

"Leaving Holland, I believed that the Pope was someone who just talked of what you weren't supposed to do," said Remery.

"In Manila, I saw a very good old person who was like a grandfather for all of us. The more I looked at him that night and the next day, the more I began to understand that he loved us."

Others probably thought so too, since the atmosphere in Rizala park that Saturday night reminded one of a family gathering more than a liturgical celebration.

"Lolek! Lolek!" chanted the young Filipinos.

146

Upon hearing the shortened version of his childhood name, the Pope said:

"Lolek does not sound serious enough. John Paul II sounds too serious. Let's try to find something in-between. Lolek is a child. John Paul II is an old man. Between the two was Karol."

These simple words evoked an even greater explosion of joy.

"Karol! Karol!" resounded the shouts.

For Michel Remery the night separating Saturday and Sunday morning was very short, yet the next day he did not feel tired. He was too preoccupied with the task the organizers had given him. He was asked to deliver a message in the presence of John Paul II in the name of the youth of the world. His heartbeat hastened when he saw the huge crowd. He was only a few feet away from John Paul II.

"I read the message during the closing ceremonies of World Youth Day in the presence of over 5 million people," recalled Remery. "Then the Holy Father asked me to approach him. We talked for a moment. I remember exactly: the Pope said that we should truly try to put the message into practice in life. He also said: 'I will pray that you will all come to know Christ and love Him all the more so that you will all be able to speak about Christ wherever you may be and no matter what might happen.'"

Michel Remery never thought then that the words of the Pope would have so much power. Today he looks at it differently.

"Maybe it was a prophecy?" he wondered. "He told me I would spread the Gospel. And now I am a priest."

At first, nothing especially pointed to a radical change in the events of his life. It is true that after returning from Manila he became more interested in his faith; he even travelled across Holland and talked to other young people about his experience. He finished his studies and began a promising professional career. He travelled to the next World Youth Day in Paris. Yet he felt a growing uneasiness. He did not know what to do, so he took a year of unpaid leave to think things over quietly. The time off ended yet he still wasn't sure. He went back to work and then it happened.

Suddenly and surprisingly, he got sick.

"It was some kind of virus," he recalled. "While I lay there incapacitated, I had lots of time to think."

He was bedridden for a whole year. He now calls those 12 months a long retreat.

"At the end of one morning I understood what I had to do," Remery said. "If I am going to be honest before God and myself, I can't be an architect – I need to be a priest. As soon as I heard ... that is, understood this information from God, I immediately tried to find reasons why I shouldn't listen to it. I tried to convince myself that I had misunderstood and that couldn't have been it at all. But after two weeks, I had to finally admit that God was asking me to become a priest. I then experienced peace. I felt that his was the right decision. Even if it was going to be hard and even if would bring much change, it was what I had to do. And I said: 'Alright, God, now we both know what you expect of me.'"

Remery entered the seminary. He was ordained a priest. I met him in Rome, where he was preparing for his doctorate. We talked a month before the death of John Paul II.

*he last time Filipinos filled the streets in such great numbers, it was to abolish a tyrant. Yesterday, however, a Pole over 70 years old brought them out with a message of hope and love.*

*Vatican officials believe that John Paul II met with the biggest crowd ever during the 17 years of his pontificate ... . The Police and the Vatican officials estimate the gathering to have been at over 4 million people; there was a million more than in 1986 when the crowd came out to face tanks and rifles in the "people power" revolution that ended the corrupt government of Ferdinand Marcos.*

*Manila Bulletin*, January 16, 1995

# EUROPE AND ASIA

On the afternoon of January 15, 1995, after the Papal Mass, a river of people carried me from Luneta Park. With other hundreds of thousands of people I walked along the streets of Manila thinking of the similarities of events in Europe and Asia.

John Paul II's visit to Poland in 1979 was a catalyst for change: it brought about the rise of Solidarity and consequently the defeat of communist totalitarianism. While we experienced months of freedom in Poland following the agreements that had been signed in August, the Pope travelled to the Far East, visiting among other places the Philippines. He was welcomed by the then dictator, Ferdinand Marcos. Marcos had declared martial law there in 1972. He ruled with an iron fist, raping the citizenry of its human rights in every way. Before the arrival of John Paul II, Marcos abolished martial law, but only as a formality. The dictator had hoped to use John Paul II's visit to strengthen his own power.

John Paul II, already briefed by the Filipino bishops, did not avoid this sensitive topic. "Appropriate concern of the authorities for the safety of the people, as is demanded for the good of all, can lead to the temptation of subordinating the individual, his dignity and his rights to the state," he said during his meeting with Marcos and the government elites at Malacanang Palace. "Every possible conflict between security needs and the basic rights of the citizenry has to be resolved according to the basic principles always put forth by the Church – that society exists only for the purpose of serving the people and protecting their dignity; it cannot claim to serve the greater good when human rights are not protected."

The Pope accomplished the first beatification in the history of his pontificate during a foreign pilgrimage: In Manila he beatified martyrs who were killed in Japan as well as a Filipino layman – a husband and a father – who found himself in Japan by accident but did not deny his faith in the face of death.

"During his first visit to the Philippines, John Paul II underlined truths and values that had decisive meaning for our people in that most difficult part of its history." That is how the legendary president of the Philippines, Corazon Aquino, would remember that pilgrimage which took place February 17-22, 1981.

Soon afterwards in the Philippines, a wave of opposition began to grow against the government of Marcos.

The local Conference of Bishops in February 1983 accused Marcos of abusing power and of corruption and warned that prolonging this situation would increase tensions further. In August Marcos's main opponent, Benigno "Ninoy" Aquino, boarded a plane flying from Taipei to Manila. For many years, Aquino had lived in political exile. When he heard of the growing resistance to Marcos, he decided to return. When asked prior to boarding the plane whether he was aware of the risk he was taking, he said: "Filipinos are worth my life."

On August 23, 1983, he arrived at Manila Airport. On the stairs descending from the plane, an assassin's bullet struck him. Aquino fell dead, leaving his wife Corazon (popularly called Cory in the Philippines) and five children. His wife was to wave to him with a yellow ribbon that she had brought to the airport. The yellow colour later became symbolic of popular resistance to Marcos.

According to the dictator's plans, the elections were spoiled – he planned to falsify them and declare himself the winner. He hoped that by this apparently democratic gesture he would appease the Americans, who were forever interested in peace in the Philippines since they had military bases there. He also wanted to bring chaos to the opposition parties, which fielded many candidates. What he did not envision was that a housewife, not a politician, would head the opposition. This housewife, as Corazon Aquino called herself, was able to unite all the opposition groups and to draw a whole nation behind her.

In accordance with the dictator's plans the election results were falsified. The Conference of Bishops in the Philippines denounced this action. After the announcement of these results in February 1986, the Minister of Defence, Ponce Enrile, and the Deputy Chief, General Fidel Ramos, together with a handful of soldiers took over Fort Aquinaldo where the Ministry of Defence was located. Ramos, and Enrile accused Marcos of falsification and years of abuse of power.

The dictator decided to squash the revolt with force. Then something happened that to this day is difficult to explain.

## THE "PEOPLE POWER" REVOLUTION

That is how those events are referred to in the Philippines.

Observers, however, preferred to refer to call it "the Philippine miracle."

One of the main players was the then Archbishop of Manila, Cardinal Jaime Sin. Some referred to him as "the Asian Richelieu," while others simply called him the Philippine Eminence; he himself liked to welcome guests with the saying: "Welcome to the house of Sin." He could get away with something like that. You could compare his authority in the Philippines with that of Cardinal Stefan Wyszyński in Poland.

A few days after the end of World Youth Day in Manila in 1995, Cardinal Sin told me this story:

"The abuse Marcos indulged in caused 152 soldiers to refuse orders, and under the constitution this meant treachery. The dictator gave the soldiers 24 hours to obey telling them: 'if you do not submit to my orders, you will be shot.' When 15 hours had passed and the revolt did not end, their wives came to me and asked me to do something or else they'd be widows. I knew that if I took steps against Marcos I would not only enrage him but I would also invite open conflict between him and the Church. What to do? The hours were passing and with them the deadline of Marcos' ultimatum.

In the meantime, I called three contemplative convents in Manila and said: 'Sisters you must leave what you are doing and go to the chapel and fast – I promised that I would fast too – and pray, because the situation is very dangerous.' Within the hour the sisters were in the chapel with outstretched arms singing *Kyrie eleison*. I thought: Now is the time to turn to the people. I did this with the help of Catholic Radio Veritas.*

I then addressed the inhabitants of Manila: 'Please leave your homes because we have to protect the lives of these soldiers.' Not even a half an hour had passed and there were more than 2 million people in the streets. They surrounded Camps Aquinaldo and Crame, where the revolt had taken place.

Marcos then ordered General Sutello to send five helicopters and drop bombs on the people and disperse the crowd. When the helicopters reached their targets, the pilots saw a live cross through the clouds. They refused to carry out the bombing and landed instead.

Today on the place where those helicopters landed in Manila there stands a chapel named the EDSA Shrine. It was at this corner that millions of people gathered together, forming what appeared from the air as a live cross. EDSA is the name of one of the streets at this corner. Each letter refers to

---

* Radio Veritas:

Radio Veritas is the largest Catholic radio entity in the world. During Marcos' dictatorship, it was the only independent media source in the Phillippines. Although in 1986 unknown parties blew up some of Radio Veritas' installations, it continued to serve as an extremely significant source of independent news.

the first letter of each word of the street name: Epiphanio de Los Santos Ave., which means Avenue of the Apparition of the Saints."

Marcos learned about the failure to disperse the crowds and decided to send in tanks.

Cardinal Sin continued:

"When the tanks got to EDSA, a beautiful woman appeared to the soldiers, who heard her say: 'Leave my people. I am the Queen of their hearts.' At that very time, the people gathered around Camps Aguinaldo and Crame were on their knees praying the rosary."

Instead of blood being spilt at EDSA, increasing numbers of Manila residents began to fraternize with the soldiers, tying yellow ribbons on the barrels of their guns – election signs for Corazon Aquino.

Meanwhile, Washington restlessly watched the development of the situation in the Philippines. Where two are fighting, the saying goes, the third benefits. Might the strong communist partisans move into action?

Cardinal Sin: "In Manila there appeared young people with red flags. They marched toward Malacanang Palace to kill the president. I told them: 'Don't do this, you will start a civil war. Stay where you are!'"

"This sounded like a command. (In fact, I was acting a bit like a commander driving about in my jeep). So they did stop. Meanwhile we called President Reagan in the United States. We told him: 'If your friend Marcos does not leave the Philippines in three hours he will be killed.' Reagan replied that Marcos could be taken to Honduras. I then said to him: "He can't go to Honduras because it isn't a good climate for him; Marcos is sick and he would not last long there. He needs special medical assistance, and he can receive this only in the United States.' Reagan's reply was short: 'Okay.' In 30 minutes, an American helicopter transported Marcos and his entourage to the Clark base, and then by plane to Hawaii."

The Global Newspaper
Edited in Paris
Printed Simultaneously
in Paris, London, Zurich,
Hong Kong, Singapore,
The Hague and Marseille
WEATHER DATA APPEAR ON PAGE 14

# Herald **INTERNATIONAL** Tribune

Published With The New York Times and The Washington Post

No. 32,041   09/86   •   THE HAGUE, WEDNESDAY, FEBRUARY 26, 1986   | ESTABLISHED 1887

No. 32,041   09/86   •   THE HAGUE, WEDNESDAY, FEBRUARY 26, 1986   | ESTABLISHED 1887

# Marcos Quits; U.S. Recognizes Aquino

### Filipinos Rejoice

# *Helicopters Signaled the End of an Era*

By Michael Richardson
*International Herald Tribune*

MANILA — An eerie silence settled around the Malacanang presidential palace late Tuesday after two U.S. helicopters lifted off of Marcos's rule. Most people are not sad that he has gone."

Mrs. Antonio and her husband, Jaime, realized that something unusual was happening about 8:30 P.M. Tuesday when they saw uniformed soldiers waved and gave peace signs.

The first two helicopters took off at 9 P.M. after Mr. Marcos, evidently realizing that he had lost his battle to stay in power, agreed in

Witnesses said that about 5,000 people swept through the ornate wrought-iron gates, pushed aside some 20 guards and forced their way into an administrative area.

The guards, marines who identi-

Headlines from the International Tribune

The following day, the *International Herald Tribune* wrote that it was impossible to list all the factors that came into play in the spectacular, bloodless overthrow of one of the longest-reigning modern dictators and the triumph of the shy and inexperienced Corazon Aquino; that the murder of her husband Ninoy set a chain reaction into motion . The rest was accomplished by "the power of the people" without force in the form of millions of Filipinos who often risked their lives to vote for her and then created a living shield to protect her and her supporters. It noted that two collaborators from the Marcos camp left him at a crucial moment; that the officer in charge of a six-helicopter attack refused an order given by the dictator and did not bomb the crowd in revolt; that the leaders of the Church and the nuns prevailed upon the madness, and that America, after initially hesitating, quickly acted and removed Marcos into exile.

Where did Cardinal Sin get the inspiration for his actions? In his own words, he admitted that he was "deeply inspired by the workers of Solidarity and the way that the Church, especially the Pope, supported this movement for the good of Poland and ultimately for the good of Europe and the world. He understood," wrote Sin, "and he always gave me courage for further action."

155

Added Cory Aquino: "Through many years, before and up till now, 'four horrible days in February 1987,' the Pope's quiet support for the decisive stand that the Philippine Bishops took after zealous prayer and deep thought was a gift and a grace for the cause of freedom and democracy in our country."

## AN ATTEMPT ON THE POPE'S LIFE

It wouldn't take much for the "Philippine scenario" to have one more thing in common with the "European scenario." The similarities didn't end with the visits of the Pope, martial law, the sudden deaths of icons for freedom (in Poland, Father Jerzy Popieluszko, and in the Philippines, Benigno Aquino) and finally transformation without bloodshed.

Not long before the Pope's second visit to the Philippines a fire broke out in the centre of Manila. One of the houses on Taft Avenue was on fire, and it was very close to the Apostolic Nunciature, which was where the Pope was to sleep. The firefighters were able to put out the fire. Inside the house they found packages that turned out to be explosive materials.

The police deduced that the residence had in fact been a terrorist base. As it turned out they found two cassocks and exact maps of the routes John Paul II would be travelling along the streets of Manila.

Inside the place they found computer discs containing a plan to murder the Pope. The terrorists knew that World Youth Day would bring great crowds. They wanted to put a bomb near the altar that would cause maximum death and planned to install snipers who would shoot into the crowd after the explosion to create even more panic.

The fire in the house on Taft Avenue was the result of a detonation inadvertently caused by one of the terrorists. This happened on January 6, 1995. The Pope arrived in Manila on January 12. On January 15, he said Mass for over four million people. The unmasking of the terrorists can be seen as a stroke of luck, one of many. One can add to it the failure of Ali Agca's gun on May 13, 1981, and the seizing of Ferdinand Krohn, who tried to stab the Pope with an army bayonet in Fatima on May 12, 1982. Also, there was the discovery of explosives under a bridge in Sarajevo one hour before the Pope was supposed to arrive in 1997. (The area had been searched earlier and nothing had been found. The police redid the search after a member of the public noticed some suspicious people loitering about the bridge.)

"I told them often," said the Pope's photographer, Arturo Mari, recalling his talks with the Pope's security personnel, "pray that nothing happens, because if it does you won't be able to handle it by yourselves. Only the Mother of God can protect him ... you definitely can't."

The disc found in the terrorists' residence in Manila, besides containing plans to kill the Pope, also had plans to attack civilian passenger aircraft. The terrorists wanted to blow up twelve Boeing 747s over the Pacific Ocean. As it turned out, the apartment had been rented to Wali Khan Shah and Ramzi Ahmed Yousef: the latter was captured by American and Pakistani forces a month later on February 7, 1995, in Islamabad.

Yousef was responsible for the attack on the World Trade Center in 1993. Some of the funds needed to proceed with their plans were received from his uncle, super-terrorist Khalid Sheikh Mohammed – the very one who at a 1996 meeting in Tora Bora, Afghanistan, gave Osama bin Laden the idea to hijack passenger aircraft and use them to destroy chosen targets in the USA.

World Trade Center, New York, September 11, 2001.

*The new millennium opened with two contrasting scenarios: one, the sight of multitudes of pilgrims coming to Rome during the Great Jubilee to pass through the Holy Door which is Christ our Saviour and Redeemer; and the other, the horrible terrorist attack on New York City, an image of a world in which hostility and hatred seem to prevail.*

*The question that arises is dramatic: on what foundations must we build the new historical era that is emerging from the great transformations of the 20th century?*

John Paul II
World Youth Day evening vigil, Toronto, July 27, 2002

World Youth Day Cross, Station of the Cross, Toronto, July 26, 2002.

# SEPTEMBER 11th

"I was then in school, unaware of what was going on. Life was beautiful. Not long before, our family had finished building its dream house... I couldn't believe this attack."

Pope John Paul II listened with great attention to the story Brennan Basnicki was telling. Brennan travelled to Rome with the rest of the Canadian delegation four months before World Youth Day, which was to take place in the country of the maple leaf. The Canadians were taking part in the yearly meeting of the Holy Father with youth in Rome. Brennan was talking about what happened on September 11, 2001. That day his father found himself in one of the World Trade Center towers.

"I thought my father, who was a very fit person, had somehow escaped from there or had been in a totally different place," said Brennan. "I didn't know what to think. As time went by I started to realize that maybe he wouldn't be coming home."

Ken Basnicki was killed under the ruins of the World Trade Center along with 3,000 other victims of the terrorist attack.

"I was in shock," recounted Brennan. "Did my father really become a victim of the greatest terrorist attack in the history of humanity? I was angry and infuriated with those who in such a cowardly way had taken my father's life. I desired revenge. However, in the next couple of days I participated in many Masses and spent many hours praying. I thought about how Jesus was persecuted and how He died for us on the cross. I thought about how the Apostles ran away and lost hope. And yet Jesus filled them with new hope when He was resurrected. God does not hide when troubles come..."

"The theme of World Youth Day is: "You are the salt of the earth, you are the light of the world". My father was the salt of the earth; his whole life was filled with the scent of the Gospel, especially in the difficult business world. He brought that scent to many people. My father was a light in the world and in my life: his goodness and his kindness, his modesty and honesty shone in the darkness and shadow of this world.

"After September 11, friends and family gathered around the whole world looking for hope. Our family received support from friends, family and even from people we didn't know. We were together and the tragedy brought us closer together than ever before. We learned to live and never give up. Sometimes our world seems senseless. In one moment we can experience tragedy and pain, sometimes great pain. But through faith, God gives us a way to live in peace and hope in a world scarred by terrorism. And this is why I am here before you today: to tell you that if you have hope, life will turn out right in the end."

Brennan gave his testimony on March 21, 2002.

On July 23 the Pope came to Toronto, and on July 27-28 he met with the youth in Downsview Park.

John Paul II greets the youth at Exhibition Place, Toronto, July 25, 2002.

*lthough I have lived through much darkness, under harsh totalitarian regimes, I have seen enough evidence to be unshakably convinced that no difficulty, no fear is so great that it can completely suffocate the hope that springs eternal in the hearts of the young.*

John Paul II,
Toronto, July 28, 2002.

John Paul II at Downsview Park during the WYD closing Mass,
Toronto, July 28, 2002

# DON'T WORRY

Father Tom Rosica had the impression that something was bothering him; there seemed to be a weight on his heart. He felt this very anxiety from the moment he began organizing World Youth Day in Toronto. The Basilian, in the third year of preparation, overcame many obstacles. Above all he had to convince everyone that the Pope, in poor health, would not be undergoing undue risks in coming to Canada. There was no short supply of figures from the media and political spheres who drew ominous images of the death of John Paul II on Canadian territory and all the complications that implied. The success of the event came under a great question mark as the number of participants began to fall after the attack on the World Trade Center. Many people were frightened to travel by plane because of the possibility of further terrorist attacks. Once the Holy Father arrived, however, it was plain to see that those fears could be easily dispelled. Two days of Papal visits near the shore of Lake Ontario and the surprising influx of youth into Toronto had transformed the city. On Saturday, July 27, 2002, more than half a million young people participated in the evening vigil with John Paul II at Downsview Park. On Sunday, the Pope was to say Mass to conclude the celebration.

In the morning, giant dark clouds gathered above the Mass site and rain poured down on the pilgrims who had spent the night sleeping outdoors. To make matters worse, Father Rosica received word from Morrow Park, where John Paul II was staying, that the wind was too strong and the helicopter might not be able to depart.

The wind had indeed intensified. Fr. Rosica looked with great anxiety at the podium where the Pope was to say Mass. A great gust of wind had torn off a huge portion of the roof which covered the biggest stage ever built on the North American continent. This allowed the rain to completely soak the waiting Bishops and Cardinals.

Through the whistling wind, Fr. Rosica heard a trembling voice from his hand-held receiver.

"Rosica," he answered briefly.

"Father, we're going to take off after all," Fr. Rosica heard.

So the Pope was coming after all! He was gladdened, and then looked at the vast scene before him. How many could there be? Half a million? 700,000? It was difficult to tell, especially since the youth hid wherever they could from the rain. Opened umbrellas, coats over their heads, tent canopies – it all formed a gigantic roof over the multitudes who had camped out there since the night before. Fr. Rosica sympathized with them for having had such a wet wake-up call. At least they were young. But what about the Pope?

The wind was still blowing and torrents of rain came down with great force when Fr. Rosica saw the helicopter approaching. Moments later, beaten by the rain and the helicopter's downdraft, he ran over to the door.

"Holy Father, I am so sorry about the weather."

The Pope smiled. He looked at the sky, stretched out his hand in the direction of the dark clouds, and blessed them.

"Don't worry," the Pope told him.


Three years after these events, Fr. Rosica's voice still trembles with emotion when he recalls that time.

"The Bishops had to hold their mitres," he recalled. "The whole stage was ready to blow away – the Mass books, the altar cloth and the chairs. Finding myself in the company of police chiefs from across most of Canada I prayed silently, begging God to help us get through this last challenge and to overcome this final hurdle. I was most surprised by the Pope, though. This old man who had seemed so weak remained calm and smiling through it all."

"For me and for many others, it was the wind of Pentecost."
Fr. Tom Rosica, CEO of World Youth Day 2002 in Toronto.

World Youth Day, Toronto. July 28, 2002. In the morning, giant dark clouds gathered above the Mass site and rain poured down on the pilgrims who had spent the night sleeping outdoors.

John Paul II at Downsview Park during the WYD closing Mass, Toronto. July 28, 2002

The wind continued to blow strongly.

The Mass began. The Holy Father recited a prayer relating to the Sacrament of Baptism.

The Pope joked that a natural baptism had rained down upon all gathered. This invoked joy among the youth, wet and cold from the weather. Though the wind became stronger, the rain began to clear. From behind the thick clouds the sun began to peak through. When the deacon began to read the Gospel, the sun shone down upon the multitudes.

"Lluvia …viento … sol," said the Pope in Spanish, which meant "rain …wind …sun."

The youth responded enthusiastically.

"It rained, it was cold, and the wind blew," recalled a reporter the following day.

"Then suddenly the Pope began to speak, the sky cleared and the sun started shining. Wow, this guy is good. I hope I'll become a better person because of him."

"For me and for many others, this was the wind of Pentecost – the one we know about from the second chapter of the Acts of the Apostles," said Fr. Rosica.

"Father, were you amazed that the weather suddenly changed?" I asked the Basilian.

"I knew that was how it was supposed to be, that God had planned it that way."

"What about the Pope? Did he make any comments about what happened?"

"He was very serene. I talked to him that afternoon. 'Your Holiness, forgive me,' I said. 'Everything was wet … it didn't turn out the way we wanted.' He laughed. 'It was fine,' he answered."

"Besides the unusual change in weather, were there any other unexplained events?"

"I know of two healings: one of a nun at Morrow Park where the Holy Father stayed, also of a young person at Downsview. But I want to tell you a different story."

# MESSENGER OF HOPE

Tony was one of 700 young people who wrote to the World Youth Day office with a request to greet the Pope when he arrived at Pearson Airport in Toronto.

"Of course we had to choose from among them, since the Pope could not talk to all of them," recalled Fr. Rosica. "I decided that we would choose Tony. He was seventeen years old and from a poor family. He became paralysed after a stroke; he had difficulty speaking and got about by wheelchair."

Thus Tony was at Pearson Airport on July 23. He watched the plane land, saw the crews bring the stairway to the door of the plane, and finally the stooping silhouette of John Paul II at the door. Fr. Rosica observed the same scene. He, especially, was amazed. He knew that a lift had been prepared to lower the Pope from the plane down to the ground. But it was obvious that John Paul II made his own decision; he would descend the stairs on his own.

"I was in shock," said Rosica, "watching the Pope struggle at every step on the way to the ground. I know that he made the decision all by himself."

About half an hour later, the greeting ceremony commenced. Tony came up to the Pope in his wheelchair. Even though their meeting was so short, it brought an amazing change in the life of this boy.

"I am in ongoing contact with him," said Fr. Rosica. "Today he can move around on his own."

Was this a miracle?

"Meeting the Holy Father was a tremendous experience for Tony, as was the sight of the Holy Father who with such great effort overcame those stairs to make it to the ground. Tony told me afterwards: 'If he can struggle that hard then so can I.'" Tony undertook difficult and strenuous therapy that demanded effort. After a couple of years, it began to bear fruit.

"I wanted to walk down those stairs to show you
that I was close to you."
John Paul II descending the stairs onto the tarmac
at Pearson International Airport, Toronto, July 23, 2002.

"Father, do you know why John Paul II made the decision to do it on his own?"

"First I'll say that when he was leaving Canada on July 29 I was lucky enough to be with him between the time he left the helicopter and boarded the aircraft. The aircraft was named *Messenger of Hope*. When we reached the red carpet, I bent over to him and said: 'Your Holiness, the elevator is ready to take you to the aircraft. Have a good trip and thank you.' He bent over towards me, thanked me, and said: 'I came down by the stairs so now I'll take the stairs up.' It literally left me speechless.

In November the Pope invited Cardinal Ambrozic (Archbishop of Toronto), Bishop Berthelet (then chairman of the Canadian Conference of Catholic Bishops) and me to dinner at the Vatican. We reminisced about World Youth Day in Toronto. At the end of the meal something unusual happened. Everyone left the dining room of the Apostolic Palace and went to St Peter's Square. I was the youngest in the group, so I was the last to say goodbye to the Pope. He held onto my hand. To my astonishment he recalled his coming down the stairs from the plane in Toronto. 'When I realized how much difficulty, struggle and tears you had to go through in order to prepare World Youth Day in Canada,' he said, 'I wanted to walk down those stairs to show you that I was close to you and that I really appreciate what all of you did. See you soon and thank you with all my heart.'"

# BISHOP TADEUSZ KONDRUSIEWICZ

# I WAS THANKFUL FOR THE HOPE THAT WE REDISCOVERED THANKS TO HIM

When Karol Wojtyła was elected to the Petrine See, he was a seminarian in Kowno, in one of only two Roman Catholic seminaries in the entire Soviet Union. He was ordained a priest three years later on May 31, 1981. On October 20, 1989 John Paul II ordained him a Bishop in St. Peter's Basilica in Rome. He was the first Roman Catholic bishop ministering in the territory of the former Soviet Union (if one doesn't count Lithuania and Latvia). Today, Tadeusz Kondrusiewicz is the Archbishop of the Roman Catholic diocese of Our Lady in Moscow. During the ordination, John Paul II reassured the newly consecrated prelate saying, "Tadeusz, don't worry, everything will go well. I am praying for you."

**Archbishop, do you truly believe that this pope really overturned communism?**

After the death of the Holy Father much was written and spoken about him in Russia: his efforts for unity, his thwarted visit to Moscow and of the fall of the Berlin Wall. The conviction continually emerged that without him, none of this would have taken place. I am personally convinced that this would not have happened so rapidly and without bloodshed.

**Do you see any link between the attempt on his life in St. Peter's Square, May 13, 1981, and the later development of events in Europe?**

Clearly this date is tied to the mystery of Fatima. It is also a well-known spiritual truth that the powers of evil always try to contradict the good. It is my conviction that these powers understood the role that John Paul II could play in this drama. In the first years of his pontificate, his engagement in the pursuit of freedom, the dignity of the human person and human rights was clear. After the assassination attempt he himself often said that it was the Mother of God who saved his life. In my opinion, the fall of the Soviet Union is linked to the message of Fatima and with what the pope did on March 25, 1984, in St. Peter's Square, during the Solemnity of the Annunciation. He entrusted the world to the Immaculate Heart of Mary. This was, as Sister Lucy would later confirm, the fulfillment of Mary's request in Fatima. This was linked to the conversion of Russia. There are other dates that evoke wonder at their connection to significant Marian Devotions in the Church. On December 8, 1991, on the Solemnity of the Immaculate Conception, the leaders of Russia, Belarus and Ukraine signed a document declaring the fall of the Soviet Union. I doubt that they consciously chose this date, but I believe that this was a sign. Then, there was Christmas of that same year. I was already in Moscow in the church of St. Louis. At the time, this was the only functioning Catholic church in the capital of Russia. On Christmas Day the Celebration of the Eucharist was to be televised from this church. A few days earlier the Italians asked to have the celebration moved up a few hours because it would clash with Mikhail

Gorbachev's televised announcement. We agreed. And so following the televised Mass, Mr. Gorbachev announced to the world the end of the Soviet Union and his own resignation.

**And Gorbachev's role?**

In 1991, even before the fall of the Soviet Union, I spoke with Sr. Lucy. She told me then that Gorbachev was a tool in the hand of Divine Providence.

**What did he think about the Pope?**

We met many times. He always spoke positively about John Paul II and often fondly recalled his meetings with the Holy Father. I recall how a journalist once said to him that he, Gorbachev, brought down the Berlin Wall. When he heard this he denied it and said, "Oh no, it was the Pope."

**When you heard that a Pole was chosen to sit on the throne of Peter, did you believe that something would change?**

I was a seminarian then. The power of the Soviet Union seemed to be enormous. We saw communism as a persisting monolith. There was no freedom of speech. In the seminary we were not even allowed to have a radio. I remember when someone brought the news that the Archbishop of Cracow was chosen as Pope. I remember how much we rejoiced that the See of St. Peter would now be lead by a Slav, someone so close to us and a man who knew this system. It was difficult at the time to imagine how the future would unfold. We were confident, however, that the one who would become Pope knew our situation well. And we knew that he would not allow himself to be deceived and that he would know what he must do.

**What is the role of the Pope? How was it possible to avoid a violent reaction and the spilling of blood? After all, even in the early 1980s, the world was divided into two blocs. There was a real danger of nuclear war. And yet the changes that took place in the Eastern Bloc proceeded peacefully...**

You ask about the role of the Pope… Well, what can I say… that God works through people. This was the right man at the right time. Above all, he defended the dignity of the human person. He spoke not only to us but *for* us. This educated and formed people of integrity. In Poland Solidarity was born and this went further east. After this came the time when people on the bottom no longer wanted to live like this, and the ones on top were powerless. Let us remember about the great faith of the Pope. Every time I spoke of the difficulties my ministry encounters in Russia he would calm me down saying, "Remember the words of the Mother of God in Fatima: 'My Immaculate Heart will triumph and Russia will be converted.'" And it seems that the truth of his words was confirmed on the day he returned to the Father's house. It was the first Saturday of the month – remember that Mary in Fatima asked for the establishment of the First Saturdays of the month – as well as the vigil of the Feast of Divine Mercy. In the Orthodox church there is a conviction that if someone dies within the first week after Easter, he goes directly to heaven. John Paul II died in this time.

**We have met you in different geographical locations on the occasion of World Youth Days. We first spoke in Manila, where there was an unprecedented 4 million people gathered for the Papal Mass. How do you recall that event?**

Well, beginning with Jasna Góra, I was at every World Youth Day. The gathering in Manila was really something incredible. I remember how we couldn't get to the place where Mass would be celebrated because the people blocked every access road. We had to walk single file, Cardinals and Bishops, through a sea of people, in order to get to the altar. When Mass was over, after arriving at the hotel, we waited a long time for Cardinal Arinze. Finally he arrived to tell us that he was unable to get there sooner because of the crowds. In the end the police had to transport him by motor-boat to the hotel, which was located along a river.

The world has never seen anything like this and it had a great impact on our young people. One could see that even surpassed the dreams of the Pope himself. A very important fact was the official presence of a Chinese delegation. For the first time in history they came to such a celebration. I believe this was very important, particularly today. I mean the efforts of Benedict XVI in trying to normalize relations with China. We know that John Paul II had an unrealized dream: a pilgrimage to Moscow and to Bejing. I think that sooner or later these pilgrimages will take place. After the last synod of bishops in Rome, I wrote an article entitled, "The Synod of Two Popes." I believe it will be the same for the pilgrimages of the successor of Saint Peter to Moscow and Beijing. Let us call them the pilgrimage of two Popes; the one here on earth and the one in heaven.

**John Paul II began his pontificate with the phrase: "Be not afraid; open the door to Christ." Entering the third millennium the Holy Father often repeated the words, "stop being afraid." How do you interpret these words?**

I am certain that papal challenge from 1978 initiated changes which resulted in the fall of the Berlin Wall. In 1991 in Rome a synod for the bishops of Europe was held. At the time many thought that the major problems were now resolved and that everything would go forward easily. There was universal enthusiasm, but time showed that things were not as they seemed. New challenges emerged along with new fears. Many people, particularly in the former eastern bloc began to experience "nostalgia." They were afraid of what the future might bring. Secularism began to make serious inroads and a new god, "mammon," appeared among us. We didn't know quite how to deal with this and we wondered what would happen to the Church. All of this gave birth to fear. The words, "stop being afraid" are from the book of Revelation and were used by the Pope in the document he wrote after the second Bishops' Synod for Europe. They were his response to the fear, and the new unease linked to new threats. The clearest sign of their presence were the terrorist attacks on the World Trade Center, as well as terrorism and violence in other countries; also in our country, in Russia, there are serious threats. The only response to these threats is to challenge the conscience of people.

**The Holy Father was fully aware of this atmosphere. When he travelled to Toronto one year after 9/11, he called the terrorist attack on New York a specific icon of the world in which hostility and hate seem to triumph. And at the same time he tried to strengthen the hearts of his audience with hope...**

Yes. I was also in Toronto and I remember that meeting well. I was most impressed by the Way of the Cross along the streets of the city. We were awestruck by the great crowds gathered in this secularized city. Later, during the night vigil at Downsview, there was a terrible rainstorm soaking the young people for Sunday. And yet they did not run away. They waited for the Pope. It was clear that they saw hope in this aged man, that they received a new spirit thanks to him.

**I, too, was particularly impressed by the rain shower, but even more impressed by the incredible wind that dispersed the storm. The sun began to shine. What did you think when you saw the unbelievable change in weather?**

One might compare the wind with the breath of the Holy Spirit. And the Pope is a man through whom the breath of the Spirit passes and acts in people. It was obvious that he was needed by the youth. It was in Koszalin in 1991 where the weather was similar and a similar wind began to blow. The Holy Father then remarked: "I thank God for this wind." And the wind is a symbol of the Spirit who brings the sun and clement weather.

**The wind blew also in St. Peter's Square during John Paul II's funeral...**

Yes. Another breath of the Holy Spirit. The words of Cardinal Ratzinger, who referred to John Paul's last blessing from the balcony of his apartment, spoke of his conviction that even now John Paul II blesses us from the window of the house of the Heavenly Father.

**Would you agree with the popular signs that read Santo subito?**

When I travelled in autumn to the Synod of Bishops on the Eucharist, I was asked to testify at for the beatification process. I said it then, albeit without a sign: Santo subito.

**How did your personal farewell with the Pope look like?**

I travelled to Rome over some fifteen hours. At the time I had to be in Moscow. I arrived at the Vatican on Thursday. Unexpectedly, I was asked to preside at the Eucharist in St. Peter's Basilica during the time when the body of the deceased Pontiff was presented for mourners. It is difficult to speak of this. [The archbishop's voice began to crack with emotion.] I had tears in my eyes. I thanked God for such a Pope, especially in the Russian context. I thanked him for the rebirth of church structures and for the hope that we all regained because of him. Tens of bishops concelebrated the Mass along with some sixty priests. I spoke about this later in Moscow and the people just couldn't believe that there were so many priests. We have very few for our needs. Then there was the great march of people. They were content to wait 10 to 20 hours to walk past the open coffin. This was a worldwide retreat. People who were standing in line would come up to me and ask for confession. I thought of it as a posthumous audience with the Pope: his lesson. What he had been striving for all his life was accomplished. He longed to see people open the doors of their hearts to Christ. And when he died, God's actions through his person became most obvious.

**Were there any unusual situations in the Archdiocese of Moscow? To put it bluntly, were there any miracles attributed to the Pope?**

Many people told me that his attitude forced them to a revision of their lives and an examination of conscience. When he died, they came back to God. Here in Moscow these experiences helped many to straighten out their family lives. Now they may once again receive the sacraments. I can also speak of the testimony of two priests. One speaks of a certain prisoner serving time in Novogrod. This man suffered from tuberculosis and was in mortal danger. After John Paul's death he began to pray through the Pope's intercession and the illness vanished completely. The other priest was struggling with incredible bureaucratic roadblocks in trying to register a newly constructed church in Orle. You know how it is in Russia. To build a church is one thing, to deal with the bureaucracy is an altogether more difficult reality. This priest called his parishioners to pray through the intercession of the Pope. The difficulties were removed in a very short time – as if a hand had lifted them.

A few days ago I received a letter from the city of St. Petersburg from a certain woman whose husband had a heart attack and had in fact experienced clinical death. The doctors' prognosis offered no hope for his brain to recover or for him to return to his normal work. On the way to the hospital his wife decided to pray to John Paul II, that her husband be given the gift of regaining his normal life. The doctor who greeted her at the entrance of the emergency ward said with astonishment that a half hour earlier (at the time of her prayer) her husband recovered consciousness and responded to questions. From a medical point of view the doctor was unable to explain what had happened. Today, her husband has returned to his former employment.

**Do you think that the many challenges facing the world on the threshold of the third millennium can be overcome in the same peaceful manner that the problems of Europe were resolved during the 1980s?**

We must take into account not only external threats such as conflicts, terrorism, social injustice, etc., but also internal ones. Above all the spread of secularism, moral relativism, a way of living as if God didn't exist. Everything is in the hands of God's Providence, in which we should place our trust. Much also depends on us, Catholics, people of faith. The world also needs our witness. I deeply believe that the memory of John Paul II, his teaching, example and trust in God through Mary, as well as the teaching and many appeals of Benedict XVI for peaceful resolution to emerging conflicts and for the establishment of moral order, will bring the hoped-for effects.

# Chapter 5.

## IN THE FATHER'S HOUSE

*N*one of us can ever forget how in that last Easter Sunday of his life, the Holy Father, marked by suffering, came once more to the window of the Apostolic Palace and one last time gave his blessing Urbi et Orbi. We can be sure that our beloved Pope is standing today at the window of the Father's house, that he sees us and blesses us. Yes, bless us, Holy Father. We entrust your dear soul to the Mother of God, your Mother, who guided you each day and who will guide you now to the eternal glory of her Son, our Lord Jesus Christ. Amen.

Cardinal Joseph Ratzinger
Homily during the funeral Mass for John Paul II
April 8, 2005

"Maybe it's better that I die if I can no longer fulfill the mission entrusted to me," John Paul II told Archbishop Stanislaw Dziwisz. On Easter Sunday, March 27, 2005, the Pope delivered his Urbi et Orbi blessing at the Apostolic Palace – but was unable to speak.

*t the request of His Most Eminent and Reverend Cardinal Camillo Ruini, Vicar General of His Holiness for the Diocese of Rome, the Supreme Pontiff BENEDICT XVI, taking into consideration the exceptional circumstances put forward during the Audience granted to the same Cardinal Vicar General on 28 April 2005, has dispensed the five-year waiting period following the death of the Servant of God John Paul II (Karol Wojtyła), Supreme Pontiff, so that the cause of Beatification and Canonization of the same Servant of God can begin immediately. Notwithstanding anything to the contrary.*

From the Congregation for the Causes of Saints,
read by Pope Benedict XVI, at the Basilica of St. John Lateran,
May 13, 2005.

# WINDS OVER
# THE YUCATAN

*Mérida, Mexico, Sunday July 17, 2005.*

Elizabeth felt fear gripping her throat. Was a similar hell awaiting them as it did in 1988 with Hurricane Gilbert? She put aside the latest edition of *The Yucatan Daily*. The headline read: "State of Emergency" and the article warned that Hurricane Emily was turning into a monster.

This was to be the final calm before the advent of torrential rains and devastating winds which were expected to arrive at around 9 p.m. The forecast was for the hurricane to last almost an entire day.

"Twenty-hours!" Elizabeth gasped. "How are we to survive?"

She began to act. She had to check to see if everything they needed was in the house. She knew there would be no electricity, so she prepared flashlights and a battery-powered radio. Thankfully, she was able to gather together supplies of food and drinking water. Together with her son, she checked the kerosene lamps and filled the buckets with water. They managed to fill the car with gas and to check if the car battery was functioning. Then they secured the windows with special tape.

They worked all day, and in the evening they were ready. Finally Elizabeth could rest and this was the most difficult. As long as she was active, she didn't have time to think of what was coming. Now that evening was at hand, and the hurricane with it, she could do nothing else. Exhausted, she sat down in front of the television set. The news announcer spoke of the coming cataclysm, the consequences of which she could picture in her mind. On the television she heard the rustle of windswept branches, a sudden crash of breaking trees and roofs ripped from their supporting walls announcing the arrival of the hurricane in the deserted streets.

She knew that the wind could hit the houses, overturn the kerosene lamps and cause spontaneous fires. She knew that after the devastation, looters could appear in the city and insects could invade houses by the thousands.

"I was terrified, I admit," recalled Elizabeth. "I was afraid of the powers of nature that arise against humans and force them to feel their might. I was afraid for my daughter who was unable to return home and remained in Cancun. I was afraid for my other children and for myself. After all, we were in the path of a hurricane! I was afraid for the residents of our city, for my house, my friends, my street and parks. I was afraid that once again I would have to look at broken trees, cables torn apart, devastated homes and rubble, like after an earthquake or bombing."

She then looked at a picture of Karol Wojtyła, which was in the room. The Holy Father had his arms lifted for blessing.

"Karol Wojtyła, whose life was a clear theophany and whose spiritual presence became for me more certain, more real, and more obvious from the day when he passed from this world – it was to him that I entrusted my fears and whom I asked for help and protection: yes, I admit it. I believed that God, Our Lord, through the intercession of His Servant would free us from all the harm and evil. And in answer to my prayers, I immediately heard him speaking to me the phrase he had repeated so many times, which he spoke also to himself in the many key moments of his life: 'Do not be afraid.' Looking at his peaceful, serene smile, I began to feel that my fear was passing, replaced by an unending trust and feeling of security."

Outside it was now completely dark. There was total silence; "a silence before the storm," Elizabeth thought. Everything

Hurricane Emily spares Mérida – satellite photo of Hurricane Emily which devastated the Yucatan Peninsula but left Mérida untouched.

was pointing to an imminent attack on the city by the ferocious wind. The municipal water was now cut off and the news announcer warned that the electricity would also be cut off soon. Hurrican Emily was moving forward. Elizabeth decided to turn the TV off and try to sleep for a while. She prayed once again to the Pope. As she was falling asleep she decided to add a promise to her prayer. "If a miracle happens," she thoughtfully decided in her heart, "I will write about this to Rome to support the cause for his beatification and canonization." At the time, I also thought that a miracle would give me certainty that my prayers were answered and that God truly loved me, gifting me with such a sign.

Finally she fell asleep and awoke around 5 a.m. She was surprised by the light flowing through the corridors. She heard the rustle of the fan and understood that the electricity was not cut off. Instead of cracked trees and devastation she saw a calm, empty street. A light drizzle was falling and it seemed that Emily had not yet arrived in Mérida. She turned on the TV and saw a satellite image of the hurricane which was passing over the Yucatan peninsula. But the characteristic image of a mounting spiral of clouds was different from the other pictures. She clearly saw an empty space precisely over Mérida and a few other towns in the southern peninsula.

The image looked like an oil painting on which the artist's finger had been passed at the last moment so as to create a small path through the clouds of the hurricane, leaving a bright, clear fragment, completely calm and quiet. Upon seeing the satellite photo, she immediately thought that Karol Wojtyła interceded and that God had performed a miracle.

The following day, her daughter phoned from Cancun and said that it was peaceful there as well.

The press reported that, as it approached the peninsula, the hurricane had great force, but abruptly lost its strength. Elizabeth was convinced that it was a miracle, "similar to the one that took place at the Red Sea when the waters parted before the children of Israel running away from the Pharaoh," she affirmed.

On Monday, July 18, the *Yucatan Daily* printed the satellite photo of Emily on the front page. The headline read "Devastating Fury." Indeed, the Yucatan was to do battle with the hurricane, but the picture clearly showed that over the city in which Elizabeth lived the skies were clear. "Emily Forgives Mérida," read the headline of the very next edition. The governor of the Yucatan, clearly astonished by the gentleness of the storm and its effects, which were far less catastrophic

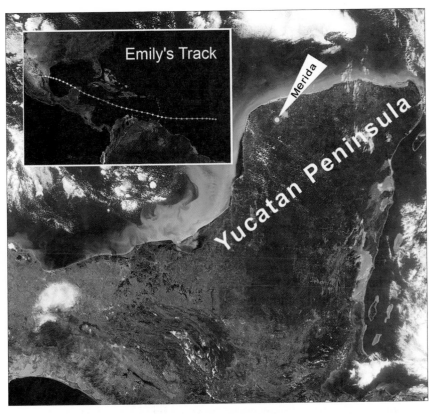

The path of Hurricane Emily.

than expected, sought an explanation: "Magic, a happy ending, a miracle and better preparedness."

In fulfillment of her promise, Elizabeth sent her testimony to Rome. She is convinced that the city was saved because of the intercession of the Pope from Poland, as are the authors of thousands of testimonies sent to Rome since April 2, 2005, the day John Paul II was born to heaven.

# CONFESSOR
# OR MARTYR?

Which, if any, of these testimonies will be the miracle, the sign from God that will affirm that John Paul II may be beatified?

Perhaps it will be the miracle that Archbishop Stanislaw Dziwisz publicly announced on November 29, 2005. On the occasion of the opening of a new chapel for the Federation of Italian Workers (ACLI), the Archbishop revealed that in France there had been a miracle attributed to John Paul II and that this miracle would be taken into consideration during the beatification process. Father Slawomir Oder, the postulator for the process of beatification of the Pope, did not reveal any details about this miracle because he is bound by a vow of confidentiality.

Such a sign will in all likelihood be needed for John Paul II to be elevated to sainthood. Why "in all likelihood?" Everything depends on how, and under what title, the Pope will be beatified and canonized. One may be declared a confessor or a martyr.

In Vatican circles, suggestions emerged that John Paul II was a martyr and that his agony during March and April of 2005 had already begun on May 13, 1981.

Prophetic words attributed to St. Padre Pio, who was beatified and canonized by John Paul II, could confirm this proposition. When he met Karol Wojtyła, the stigmatic was alleged to say, "Greetings to the future Pope and Martyr." Is this only a legend or is there some truth in these words? Karol Wojtyła and Fr. Pio spoke in 1947 at San Giovanni Rotondo. It is certain that the future Pope went to confession to the Capuchin priest, and it is universally known that in 1962 Bishop Wojtyła asked Fr. Pio for prayers for Wanda Półtawska, a co-worker suffering from cancer. Półtawska recovered from the cancer, and Fr. Pio ordered the letter of thanks written by Bishop Wojtyła to be kept, saying, "Someday this letter will have great significance." Did he already know that this Pole from Cracow will be Pope? If so, perhaps he also knew about his martyrdom?

All of this is only speculation. Fr. Slawomir Oder is of the opinion that acknowledging John Paul II as a martyr is highly unlikely. He feels that too much time passed from the time of the assassination attempt and the Holy Father's death. "It seems to me that some speak of a 'process of martyrdom' because in such a process a miracle is not needed," clarifies Fr. Oder. "Martyrdom, however, is considered a miracle in itself. The choice of this path – a process acknowledging John Paul II as a martyr – could certainly shorten the time for the canonization process."

The cult of the martyrs reaches back to the early centuries of Christianity when the faithful of the Church suffered numerous persecutions. In later ages, the term "white martyrdom" appeared, signifying a heroic life dedicated to God ending with natural, not sudden, death. In order to determine if the life of the candidate for canonization did indeed have this character, a meticulous presentation of evidence must occur. After this, a confirming sign from God in the form of a miracle is needed. Only after this can the Pope decide to pronounce the candidate "blessed." For canonization another miracle is needed. Most often it is a miraculous healing, since it is the easiest to document. Of course, the miracle must occur after the death of the one the Church is hoping to canonize. There are many testimonies to such miraculous healings, and some are well known.

# A CHILD, WORK AND A GOOD EAR

 Leticia Sales De Bores lives in Ciudad Celaya in Mexico. Like hundreds of thousands of others, she spent the first days of April 2005 in front of the TV tracking the news related to the deteriorating health of the Pope. After his death the television showed many programs related to the Holy Father, one of which was an interview with a woman at St. Patrick's Cathedral in New York. The woman claimed to have received a miracle for her child thanks to the Pope. It was to have taken place during the last visit of the Pope to Mexico. The woman's daughter, whose name is Carol Georgina, could not conceive a child for the past two years. After the Pope's visit she gave birth to a daughter, also named Carol Georgina.

Under the influence of this interview Leticia Sales De Bores also decided to ask the Pope for a favour.

"I had the great fortune of seeing the Pope a number of times," she recalled, "including during World Youth Day in Buenos Aires. From the evening when he died, I began to pray before his picture which I had taken photographing the TV screen during his last visit to Mexico. Our Lady of Guadalupe is also in the picture. I prayed in these words: 'Blessed John Paul, the request of the other woman was a simple one since her daughter was married only two years earlier. My request is far more difficult since my daughter is now married fourteen years and still she is unable to conceive a child... Just as the Most Holy Virgin has you in her womb, so I long to see my daughter with a child.'"

On May 31 Monica Bores Sales, Leticia's daughter, underwent a pregnancy test which came out positive. The doctor confirmed the diagnosis on June 4 and the whole family found out that Monica was pregnant.

From the end of 2004, Germán Rodrigo Chujfi from Cartago Valle in Colombia suffered from an inflammation of his right leg. Around his knee a lump appeared, which grew in size and in the pain it caused him. Chujfi was an auto mechanic and the lump made his job very difficult. The family doctor said that it could be removed surgically, but warned that the wound from the operation will be painful for some time. He recommended that the surgery be delayed until the patient had less work. In the meantime, the lump grew to four centimetres in diameter.

"During the week when the Holy Father, John Paul II, died, the illness was difficult to bear because the lump grew and became even more painful," said the Colombian. "I spoke with the doctor who counselled me to visit an orthopedic surgeon to schedule the surgery. That same day my relative, Ruby Bueno, phoned to tell me about a 'prayer chain for the Holy Father' which was to take place at noon. We participated in the prayer with the whole family. Later a friend phoned me. She knew of my sickness and said: 'Why don't you ask the Holy Father for health? He is doing many miracles.' Her words were just what the doctor ordered, and that very night, before turning in, I prayed and asked for a resolution to my health problem. The very next day I woke up early in the morning, to find to my astonishment that the lump had disappeared."

 Jennifer of Baltimore, Maryland (USA), writes about her two-year-old son Andrew Joseph, who was born with many health problems. He had already been baptized at the hospital because of his ill health. In May 2005, the doctors informed the parents that the child's hearing was threatened because of an inflammation in his ear. "I prayed to Pope John Paul II, to save my son from this sickness and to heal his ears," testified Jennifer. "The next time we met with the specialist to discuss further treatment, the doctor declared: 'I don't know what to say. His ears are in great shape!'"

These and other testimonies can be found on the website for the beatification and canonization of John Paul II. On that site there is one more story.

## WAITING FOR A MIRACLE

Sally Sprague lives in Bloomington, Illinois. Her twenty-year-old daughter Maggie was pronounced clinically dead when her heart stopped in August 2004. The doctors managed to resuscitate her but she suffered from a prolonged lack of oxygen to the brain. "She can't walk, speak or take care of herself, but she smiles and has feelings," wrote her mother. She had a tracheotomy and is nourished by a feeding tube. Maggie is a beautiful girl, the second of four children," her mother proudly affirms. "Her illness was very difficult for her father, for me and for her two brothers and sister, as well as for her many relatives, friends and many others."

"This past spring, Maggie's health deteriorated. She had to be hospitalized and we thought she would not make it. This happened during the Terry Schiavo incident and at the time the Pope died. In the hospital room where Maggie lay, I was watching TV. They were speaking about the health of the Pope. Maggie suffered from an inflammation of the cerebral nerves which developed into a severe infection due to the poor functioning of the heart. She had a tracheotomy with a feeding tube and a breathing tube attached. She also suffered from lack of adequate oxygen to the brain, just like Terry Schiavo. While I watched the TV, I was surprised by the similarity of what both Terry and the Pope were suffering and how it was the same with my daughter. I don't know why God allowed me to feel calm and peaceful, but that's what I felt. When the Pope died, I told my husband that we should pray to the Holy Father and to Terry Schiavo, to intercede to Jesus for our beloved Maggie. After this our relatives arrived. They also said they were asking the Pope to intercede with Jesus for Maggie.

"On Wednesday, August 10 (one year after Maggie's heart attack) we had Mass offered in our home. We asked God to continue to bless us. We thanked him for Maggie's life and we asked him to heal her, since this was our only hope. The priest, who celebrated the Mass, used a chalice blessed by – and even used by – John Paul II. Maggie was able to drink from this chalice and could receive communion regularly.

I can't speak about a miracle yet. If this will be the will of God, John Paul II will intercede for Maggie. I wanted you to know this story. God allows many situations in which we see his hand and loving grace.

Please pray for us. Thank you for reading this.

I hope to add Maggie to the list of miracles attributed to our beloved Holy Father.

Thank you.

*Sally Sprague, Bloomington, Illinois (U.S.A)*